BUILDING A FAMILY BREAKS MY HEART

Based on an extraordinary
true story
by Tanika Dillard

BUILDING A FAMILY BREAKS MY HEART

Building A Family Breaks My Heart
by Tanika Dillard
ISBN-13: 978-0692397374
ISBN-10: 069239737X
First Print August 2014
10 9 8 7 6 5 4 3 2 1
Copyright © 2014 by Tanika Dillard
LIBRARY OF CONGRESS CATALOGING IN PUBLICATION
Dillard Publishing

PUBLISHER'S NOTE
This book is based on a true story. Names, characters, places, and incidents are real. Any resemblance to actual persons, living or dead, business establishments, or locales have been changed to protect those involved.

All rights reserved. No portion of this book may be reproduced, stored in or introduced into retrieval system, or transmitted in any form or by any means (electronic, mechanical, photocopy, recording or otherwise), without the prior written permission of the copyright owner and Dillard Publishing.

The scanning, uploading, and distribution of this book via the Internet or via any other means without the permission of Dillard Publishing is illegal and punishable by law.

… BUILDING A FAMILY BREAKS MY HEART

BUILDING A FAMILY BREAKS MY HEART

by Tanika Dillard

Dedication

    This book is dedicated to every mother and father who knows the longing for a pregnancy, those who have experienced pregnancy loss (es). Especially for those who still hope, dream, and believe for a family even against all odds.

    A sincere dedication to our precious children Destiny, Briauna, Madison, Ethan, Israel Grayson, and Evan, who are the products of the love that Chris and I share for each other. Their lives are the heartbeat of each page.

In memory of my beloved Grandmothers
Alma M. Smith
&
Rachel L. Chancellor

Acknowledgements

Thank you to the following individuals who without their contributions and support this book would not have been written: Tabitha Butler, Alfreda Coleman, Mikaela Davis, Patricia Henderson, Pastor Wendell Jones, Yasmin Kearse, Nikole Morgan, and Jakitta Sullivan for challenging me to get this story out of my head and onto paper.

Professional photography provided by Stephenie Robinson.

Philip Greig, MD., Arthur F. Haney, MD., Thomas Roesch, MD., and Dr. Jemine Wayman for your medical guidance and support.

Cindy Bishop and Susan Brown: Thank you for being an integral part of our family. Your passion for fragile lives and grieving families has changed our lives.

To my mother, Barbara Chancellor, thank you for your unending support and encouragement in our quest to build a family.

Most importantly, Christopher E. Dillard: My husband, lover, supporter, and friend. Your love has sustained me and given me reason to believe. Thank you for the depth of love that you've deposited into my life. I am honored to love and be loved by you.

Foreword

As a Maternal Fetal Medicine specialist for over 20 years, I have cared for many patients who have experienced the pain and utter sorrow that surrounds the loss of a child during pregnancy. I now understand that the loss of a fetus is the same to a mother as the loss of a child of any age. Even though I have been a witness of this pain so many times, and experienced the pain of my patients, it is difficult to really know what they are going through.

Tanika Dillard conveys in this book, the raw emotions of this terrible journey only a parent that experiences it can know. She does an extraordinary and courageous job in helping us look through the eyes of the heart of a family going through catastrophic loss. I know this author's personal journey is the basis of this book.

This story will be a blessing to mothers and families experiencing similar hurt. Readers will know they are not alone in their feelings and there is hope for the future. The author's description of what it is like to lose a child gives the audience a full, emotionally deep feeling for what it is like to lose a baby. She also helps us understand what to say and not say to a grieving parents. She instructs us that a long hug, a listening ear, and love are the most needed medicines to help the heart heal.

Tanika Dillard has taken repeated tragedies that would have broken most of us and turned pain into healing for many other families experiencing similar misfortunes through starting support groups and ministering to other mothers. I have learned so much from Tanika's experiences that have helped me better care for patients experiencing the heartbreaking loss of a child.

I have never cared for a patient who has experienced more pain and tragedy in trying to raise a family than The Dillard's. Yet, she has also shown more strength, faithfulness and compassion than I thought possible. I strongly recommend this book for anyone who cares for pregnant women and especially family and friends of those who have experienced this kind of loss. I hope that you will be encouraged and inspired by the strength and love of the author and her family.

Dr. Phillip Greig
Upstate Maternal Fetal Medicine

Chapter 1
I Want To Be Like You

Growing up, I can remember spending my preschool days and summers with my dear Grandma Alma while my parents worked. Paying for summer camp for three kids wasn't in the budget, and Grandma wouldn't settle for us being anywhere else. My grandmother was a beautiful soul inside and out. Standing barely five foot five inches tall, she had a hearty build with a heart that seemed larger than life.

My two older sisters, Tina and Myra, and I looked forward to being at her house – it was our home away from home. Each day we'd arrive shortly after seven o'clock and find her in the kitchen making us a hot breakfast. My sisters greeted her with a kiss, but I would have to steal at least a dozen more and her cocoa brown face seemed to beam with joy at our presence.

My Grandma's house was always peaceful and quiet. The television would be off, the windows open and the red curtains gently swaying in the cool breeze. The smell of sausage filled the air as she made my favorite meal of grits, grape jelly, and scrambled eggs, combined together on one of her brown and white plates. Some days we'd arrive with a box of corn flakes and a gallon of milk to give Grandma a break from cooking, but she quickly reminded us that she didn't mind cooking for us. Serving a hearty, well-prepared meal was an act of love in her eyes. And to show our appreciation, we left nothing on our plates but the paint.

"What are we going to do today?" Myra asked while eating her breakfast.

"I need to go to the garden before it gets too hot and pick some tomatoes and green beans," Grandma replied.

"Can we help you?" Myra asked with excitement.

Myra loved gardening. I, on the other hand, had no intention of helping assist Grandma outside in the heat. Since Tina was eight years older, she was able to spend the afternoons with her friends. However, the immediate item on my agenda was an extended nap to make up for waking up extra early. Grandma should have taken a nap as well, because by lunch time her head would slowly ease down to rest on her chest. Her gold-framed glasses would begin to roll off of her nose. "Grandma, what are you doing?" Tina asked in an effort wake her up.

"I'm just taking a little cat nap," she chuckled.

"Can we play in your hair?" I inquired. The texture of her hair was like woven silk – notably different than our thick, puffy hair. "Grandma, how did you get hair like this?"

"My father was a full-blooded Cherokee Indian and had beautiful, long, jet black hair. I reckon I got it from him. My hair used to be thick like yours, but I'm old now. Most of it's gone and the little that's left is turning white."

"Can I put these in your hair?" I said reaching for her bobby pins on the kitchen table.

We would lie in her lap and she would put our hair in two braids or freshen up the pony tails. Her polyester skirt was more comfortable than any cozy recliner. Something about Grandma's hands in my head lulled me to sleep. She used to hum a hymn while I rubbed the warm, flabby skin under her arm. "Baby, wake up and go get on Grandma's bed," she whispered as she nudged me to an upright position. She followed me to the room and covered me in her hot pink and burgundy afghan. "You comfortable?" she'd ask before walking out of her bedroom.

"Yes ma'am, I'm fine."

"Alright Sweetheart, I'll be in the kitchen when you wake up." Curled into a fetal position, I closed my eyes tightly and tried to replay the dream that started when I slept on her lap. In my dream I was a mother to a little girl named Jackie and tried to emulate everything Grandma had done for us, especially her hair.

We had such a carefree life at Grandma's, and often ran through the clothes that were neatly hanging on the clothes line just to smell the scent of her bleach and laundry soap. She would respond to our mischief with laughter rather than scold us. Our days were filled with love and great affection.

My grandparents were married for over forty-eight years before Granddaddy died of cancer in 1977, a year before I was born. So, I only knew my grandmother as matriarch of the family, but heard many stories about Granddaddy over the years. They had twelve children and four generations of grandchildren. I often held Grandma's hand and tried to identify the many colorful stones on her Mother's ring. It was absolutely beautiful. There were four rows of stones across and three rows of stones going down. I would ease the ring off her hand and quickly place it onto my index and middle fingers and pretend it was mine. There were three sapphire stones and I only knew that because it's my birthstone. "Grandma, who are the blue stones for?"

"Those are for your aunts, Emma, Bessie, and Louise; they were born in September."

"Oh, who is this one for?" pointing to the light blue stone.

"This stone is for your Momma; it's called aquamarine."

"Can I have this ring?" I asked in a bouncy voice.

"No, Sweetheart. One day you will have children and you can get a ring just like this one."

Although there were twelve stones in her ring, there weren't twelve children. Grandma knew the pain of loss and loneliness. Not only did she bury her husband, but also three of her seven sons. Her nearly two-month old son Joseph was in his bassinet beside her when he died. He had colic for several days and during one night Joseph began his usual cry of discomfort, which surprisingly ceased after a few moments. Grandma took full advantage of the opportunity to sleep while Joseph slept. By four o'clock in the morning, she jolted from her sleep because Joseph didn't wake for his usual three o'clock feeding. She lifted him from the bassinet, but his body was cold and limp. She quickly turned on the lamp to find Joseph swollen and bruised. To Grandma's surprise, a small diamondback rattlesnake was coiled at the bottom of the bassinet, robbing little Joseph of his life.

Grandma never forgot her baby boy and every year she would carefully climb the hill to the cemetery of her home church where Joseph, Granddaddy, and her other sons Otis and Melvin were buried. Several times a year she would place flowers on their graves, especially on Father's Day and Christmas.

The little house on McCray Drive overflowed with love, robust laughter, and great southern-style home cooking. We never had small, quiet family gatherings. Our Thanksgiving meals were the pinnacle of our time together. There were always numerous calls between the siblings to decide who would prepare which menu items and what time we would eat. My aunts and uncles would travel from Vermont to surprise Grandma for the holidays. We'd all gather, give thanks, eat, sing, tell stories, eat again, and enjoy the richness of the moment as we shared generations of love.

Grandma's faith in God was notable; her Bible was always within arm's reach. The pages were colorful from highlighting the Scriptures she found to be foundational for her Christian belief. I would hear her pray aloud daily, reciting the 23rd Psalm and other verses from memory. She and her friend Ethel would have devotion over the phone everyday at six in the morning. Grandma's faith and consistency in her relationship with God made me want the same. She'd wash dishes while looking out of her kitchen window singing hymns in a rich, soulful alto tone. I used to sit at her kitchen table and watch her head tilt to one side as she swayed to the rhythm of the music. Many times she would have tears falling from her face. "Grandma, why are you crying?"

"I just sang myself happy," she replied with a warm smile.

Of course, I didn't know what she meant at the time, but I gathered she was happy and that's all that mattered. I'd sit in the corner of her living room on her heater mounted to the floor and sing one of her favorite songs about trusting the

Lord. Even at the age of four or five, I knew what I was saying and wholeheartedly believed every word. It was my declaration that I would depend on and hope in the Lord until the day I take my last breath. Before I knew it, I was singing myself happy too!

Grandma often marveled at the purity and conviction she heard in my voice. She knew that despite anything I faced, I'd trust in the Lord. Grandma had a prophetic insight on many things and would share her dreams with us and warn us if she sensed danger. Growing up I was completely smitten with my grandmother and wanted to be just like her. I wanted to be a mother and eventually the matriarch of the family.

Ultimately, I wanted to be a grandmother so I could impact the lives of my grandchildren just as she had made such a difference in mine. For as long as I could remember I proclaimed to everyone that I wanted nine kids and believed that having nine children would give me a ring almost as beautiful as hers. I concluded that if Grandma could give birth to twelve children in the mid 1930s, surely I could manage nine children in this day and age. I had to be a mother and have a big family. I had to have a multitude to love and care for, especially during the holidays, and lots of family members to take care of me when I became feeble. She made my heart smile, and I knew at a very young age how it felt to love and be loved.

Grandma had multiple strokes over the years. However, the magnitude of the stroke in June of 2000 was catastrophic. While recovering from that debilitating event, she was also diagnosed with stage four cancer. For the first time in nearly twenty two years, I saw my grandmother weak and in need. Her mental capacity started to diminish a few years prior, but she was still able to function independently.

Grandma's sense of humor never faded, despite obvious signs of dementia. The stroke left her paralyzed on her left side. Comfort measures were our only option, her eighty-six year old body wouldn't tolerate the lethal doses of chemotherapy necessary to combat her aggressive cancer.

One thing was certain: Grandma would never have to darken the doors of a nursing home. There were plenty of helping hands in the family to see to it that she was well taken care of. Grandma was surrounded by her daughters, daughters-in-law, sons, and grandchildren. We filled her little house and her last days with love. Grandma knew she was dying. We all knew, but didn't want to believe what our eyes beheld. Maybe her doctor really was "wacko," as she had been telling us for years.

By early August, Grandma was confined to her home hospice bed. She was in pain, but she didn't complain even when her voice was reduced to a whisper. I didn't want to miss one word, so I would put my ear close to her lips. Each day I sat by her bedside and read the sacred Scriptures she had so colorfully highlighted in her Bible. I read the first few words from the book of John, *"Let not your heart be troubled..."* and she immediately took over and started reciting the passage in its entirety. Her weak, raspy voice reverberated with power and excitement. She made sincere efforts to sit up in the bed. Speaking those holy words strengthened her, but her paralysis prevented her from doing so. "Come on in, Jesus, hear me! Come on in, Jesus," she said as she lifted her right hand towards the door.

"Grandma, do you see Jesus?" I asked.

"Yes," she replied.

"What does He look like?"

"He looks like Jesus!" she said reverently as she rested her chin on her shoulder.

My eyes filled with tears, and a smile framed my face. I recognized in that moment she was ready to meet her beloved Savior. She faced death with such grace and assurance of her eternal home. Not many days later our family stood watch by her bedside. The white bedroom was filled to capacity. Grandchildren lined the hallway in silence and others braved the August heat by standing outside.

Grandma's eyes were fixed and her breathing was noticeably shallow. One by one, we said our goodbyes. Tina leaned over and whispered, "I love you Me-ma," in her ear and paused as if to wait for Grandma's usual reply of "I love you too, Sweetheart." Tina's eyes were glassy as she turned toward the door shaking her head "no" in dismay. She placed her hand over her mouth to muffle the breaking of her heart which presented in the form of weeping.

My strong, robust uncles discarded their pride of manhood and wept as they stroked her soft hair and kissed her pale face. Our hearts raced as hers was slowly coming to one final stop. "I think it's time," Aunt Johnnie said in tears.

We all tightly gathered in her room to send her off with singing, just like she had requested. Our hands were gripped together like the linked chain that we spoke of each Thanksgiving. We sang her favorite song, which spoke of the happiness of laying down burdens, the glorious meeting of our Savior, and reuniting with loved ones who had transitioned into eternity.

Grandma's bedroom sounded like a band of angels making a grand entrance. We had no musical instruments other than the melodies in our hearts and the tapping of our feet on the carpet. As we sang "Precious Lord," tears filled our eyes, but heaven was on our heart. With trembling voices we saw Grandma try to mouth the words along with us.

The hospice nurse pulled some tissue from her white jacket pocket and wiped tears from her own eyes as she checked for a pulse one final time. She gently rubbed Grandma's arm and shook her head – there was no pulse. As we sang, the Lord heard us and took Grandma's cancer ridden, paralyzed body to the beautiful place she had sang about, read about, and longed for.

While there was open sobbing, I slipped away into the cold bedroom across the hall and rejoiced without restraint. Grandma was instantly better, healed, and whole. My heart was heavy, but I knew Grandma was doing the same thing at that very moment as she looked upon the face of her Savior. It is extremely complex to convey the beauty of her death with words alone. In fact, I never knew that death had splendor, but I was certain that I had unquestionably experienced its majesty. Her passing was the purest, most powerful transition I ever beheld. *'Oh Death, where is thy sting?'* Grandma's death was beautifully glorious. She had not lost her battle with cancer. She had won victory over death and what a victory it was!

Even the hospice nurse noticed the grandeur of her transition. "Thank you all for allowing me to be a part of such a heartfelt passing. I see death often and many face it alone. It's not this peaceful, but this was indeed sacred. You all have a wonderful family."

The gathering of loved ones, church members and the multitude of people that had been touched by Grandma's life filled Mt. Hebron, our family church, for her home going celebration. There was standing room only for our family in the church and that was not enough space. Grandchildren and great-grandchildren were escorted to the basement because there wasn't another inch of wall space left to stand. I surveyed the audience of supporters as they swiftly fanned to cool off. There was an overwhelming sense of pride just knowing that I was connected with such a great name as Alma Roosevelt and the legacy of faith and love that she imparted.

Pastor Morris gave remarks and told us to hold our heads up high because we were kin to God's royalty. I believed his words and imagined Grandma with an extravagant crown on her head and I agreed with an echoing, "Amen."

During the funeral I didn't shed a tear. It wasn't that I was in denial about her death. In fact, I was keenly aware of the finality of her departure. Instead of crying, I chose to recall all of the wonderful memories that flowed through my mind. I realized as long as I was alive, parts of Grandma would live on, for she was an integral part of building my dream of becoming a wife, a mother, and a grandmother. Death could not destroy my foundation.

I wanted to live like Grandma and die in my old years just like she did, surrounded by generations of my children and my children's children. Little did I know that my journey to become like hers, one of building a family, would break my heart and lead me through valleys of highs and lows, gains and losses, and questionable moments when I pondered if I would ever trust God again.

Chapter 2
Previews Of Pain

As I got older, I considered myself to be a loyal friend. Keeping secrets, giving advice and helping my friends through some of their most difficult days seemed to be a natural gift for me. One of my classmates lost her mother during our sophomore year and another classmate delivered her twin sons prematurely. Shortly after they were born, they passed away. Then another one of my dear friends had an early pregnancy loss. Death and grief never frightened me, mainly because I saw death from a distance. Although I wasn't close to my classmates who had experienced loss, I grieved for them because they were hurting.

Abby, one of the teenagers I mentored as a college student came from a good home and hardworking family. She was naive in many ways and only saw the good in everyone. I was asked by her mother Mrs. Gene to mentor her after she had been involved in a brawl. Though the incident could have landed her in juvenile detention, she wasn't a bad kid. She just lacked self-esteem and wanted to blend in with the crowd.

Our relationship was more than that of a mentor and mentee. Abby was more like a curious, nerve-wracking little sister. She told me all her secrets and asked my advice on everything: career, food, fashion, relationships and anything else she could imagine. "Tee, I think I'm ready to have sex," she brought up in one of our conversations.

"Abby, you are only fourteen; you're not ready for sex. I can assure you of that, ma'am," I said sternly.

"No, really – I am ready. I want a baby too. I've always wanted one," she innocently laughed.

"A baby?! Where did that bright idea come from? You are still very much a baby yourself. You still live at home with your parents and don't have a car. You still have to finish high school and go on to college. How can you possibly be responsible enough to have a baby? And besides, your daddy would kill you twice if he knew you were even thinking like this."

There was a long pause before she replied, "I don't know, Tee, I just know that I want both of them – and I want them now."

I knew I had a lot of work to do. We had repeat conversations about sex and the many reasons to abstain. Abby trusted that my advice was with her best interest in mind. I never worried if she would make the right decision after we had an in-depth dialogue about any matter. After a few months, talks about sex and a baby were nonexistent. Abby's focus had shifted to running for vice president of her tenth grade class and joining the swim team.

I was so proud of the responsible young lady that was blossoming before my eyes. Abby campaigned for the student body seat with excitement, but lost by a very small margin. I received a text message from Abby just before I left for work one Friday afternoon that read, *"I did not win the election today."*

When I started to text a response, I thought it better to call her instead. Abby answered on the first ring. "Hey, Tee!"

"Hey! I'm sorry about the election results, but you campaigned hard and I'm proud of you for trying. You can always try again next year."

"Thank you. I had fun, but I think I'll try something new next year," she said in a shallow voice.

"What are you doing tonight? I thought I would take you out to dinner to celebrate your hard work with this process," I asked.

"That'll be perfect, because I need to talk to you anyway," she responded.

"Alright, let me call your mother to make sure it's okay and we'll go from there. In the meantime, think about where you want to go."

"Okay, but you should already know I want to go to our regular spot – I want pizza," she said with a typical teenager attitude. As I hung up the phone, immediately I wondered what Abby wanted to talk about. Surprisingly, she wasn't upset about her defeat, but seemed rather relieved that all of the campaigning and attention were over.

We arrived at Ronnie's House of Pizza for the usual favorite: barbeque chicken pizza. "Hey! I haven't seen you ladies in a few weeks! Welcome back," Krissy the waitress said with a smile. "Are y'all having the usual tonight with water and sweet tea?"

"Right again, Krissy," we laughed.

"Alright, I'll get the barbeque chicken pizza going and be right back with your drinks."

"Ms. Krissy, I think I want the buffet tonight. I'm starving," Abby requested.

Krissy and I both looked at Abby and said, "I can't believe you aren't getting your favorite pizza!!!"

"I don't want that today for some reason. I'll just have the buffet tonight."

"Well, I guess I need to order something else since I can't eat a large pizza by myself."

"Do you need a menu?" Krissy asked.

"No, I'll just have a personal pepperoni pizza with a salad and spicy ranch dressing."

"Okay, help yourself to the bar and I'll get this order going," Krissy said and walked away.

Abby hopped from her seat, went directly to the buffet and returned with a plate full of salad and another plate full of pizza. "And just where do you plan on putting all that food, ma'am?" I asked, remembering she didn't want pizza.

"Trust me, I'm going to eat all of this – I'm starving!" Abby blessed the food and wasted no time throwing the pizza in her mouth. "Tee, I need to tell you something, but I don't know how you are going to respond," she said while chewing.

"Just say it, girl – I have never known you to be at a loss for words. What's going on? Does this have something to do with the election?"

"No, it's not about the election, it's something else," she laughed.

My mind started to race as I thought about what could be on Abby's mind this time. Her mind was always on something that usually ended up being nothing that sound advice couldn't resolve. "So, are you ready to talk about it?"

"Umm, I guess. Let me get another piece of pizza and then I'll tell you." Abby took her sweet time at the salad bar before returning to the table. "Tee, promise me you won't be mad when I tell you this," she begged.

"I can't promise you that," I said with a laugh.

"Okay, so would you be mad at me if I told you I didn't want to go back to Lincoln High next year?"

"Why would I be mad about that? What's going on to make you want to change schools?"

Abby laughed and dropped her head. "So, um, I probably could still go to Lincoln, but how would I do that with a baby?"

"What do you mean, how would you do that with a baby?"

"I mean, how would I go to school with a newborn?" she repeated.

"You wouldn't! You're not having a baby until you graduate from high school, college and get married!" I said with a stern look. I wanted her to know I meant business.

There was a long pause while Abby slurped the last ounce of soda. She finally stopped her ravenous eating and reclined in her seat. "Is there anything else you want to talk about?" I asked.

"Nothing – except for the fact that I'll be having a baby in about seven months."

Abby's matter of fact tone caught me off guard. Then she put her hand over her face and started to cry. "Abby listen to me! Calm down! Are you telling me you're pregnant?"

"Yes, that's why I was secretly hoping I didn't win the election. I found out a few weeks ago after I missed my period. We had already started campaigning and I didn't want to be called a quitter. Tee, are you mad at me?"

"No Abby, I'm not mad, but I am terribly disappointed in the choices you've made. Have you told your parents yet?"

"I told them last night and they're disappointed in me also. Daddy wanted me to go to college and be successful just like he did. I can still do those things and I will, even with a baby."

Despite an extremely high risk pregnancy and many hospital admissions, Abby delivered a healthy, beautiful, vibrant son named Miguel. We didn't realize how much of a natural nurturer she was. Motherhood had its challenges, but without question she was an amazing mother.

One afternoon I received an unexpected call from Abby while I was in my office. I listened intently trying to decipher her words, but most of what I heard was sobbing. I immediately left work and rushed to her apartment. On the way I prayed fervently that I had misheard her over the phone. When I arrived at the house, she sat in shock on her bedroom floor, surrounded by her mother and Pastor Williams. The fear of what I heard was now a reality. Abby's three week old son had passed away in his sleep.

After the autopsy was complete, we learned that his death was due to undetected pneumonia. I did not know exactly what to say, but a thousand thoughts raced through my head. Why? Why Abby? Why did she come through such a high risk pregnancy to suffer this magnitude of pain? Why her innocent, beautiful son? Abby retold the events of her afternoon which concluded with putting Miguel in the bassinet for a nap and her climbing in her bed for a nap also.

There were no answers to these questions. However, I knew I had (and wanted) to be right there for her. We shopped for a dress and shoes to wear to the graveside service and took care of other necessary tasks. As we drove in silence, Abby gazed out of the window as if she was searching for something, or perhaps it was to hide the tears that fell from her face. "Are you okay?" I asked patting her knee.

"Yeah, I just feel so lost without him. This seems like it's my fault," she said.

"Absolutely not, Abby – we all know you would have never done anything to hurt Miguel. Everyone knows how much you loved him. You would have done anything to save him had you known he was sick. Sometimes things just happen beyond our control and we'll never know the reasons why."

In my encouragement, I wanted to think that my words were helping her but in reality, I felt inadequate. I had never been so close to anyone who was hurting so badly and had no idea how it felt to lose a child. And I certainly didn't know how to make it better. The more I spoke about her love for Miguel, the more she cried. There was a lump in my throat all day as I rehearsed several sympathy lines while I drove to the service. *"Abby, it was a beautiful service..."*

"Abby, I'm here for you..."

"You are strong and you're going to get through this..."

"You're in my prayers...blah, blah, blah."

Not a single one of those lines touched my heart, and I was fairly certain that it wouldn't touch Abby's fragile heart either. I didn't want to give her empty words, but wanted her to know that I hurt with her and was committed to doing anything in my power to help her as she faced each day without Miguel.

I arrived at Haven of Rest Cemetery early just to collect my thoughts. A crowd of mourners had already assembled as we waited for Abby and her immediate family to arrive. There was a special place reserved for babies and children at the cemetery called Paradise Garden. There was great pain in my heart as I saw the many headstones and faded flowers of precious children who had died. The heaviness in my heart and the thoughts in my mind didn't feel anything like paradise.

I walked by the tiny white coffin, which looked no larger than a personal storage cooler to say an official goodbye to Miguel. He was so beautiful and so perfect, just as I remembered him from the last time I saw him. He looked so peaceful lying in the cushioned casket dressed in a blue linen outfit. "Sweet dreams Baby boy, sweet dreams," I whispered as I slowly walked past his body.

Just minutes before three o'clock, silence filled Paradise Garden at Haven of Rest. The limousine carrying Abby and her family had arrived. The birds hushed their singing and the wind ceased to blow as if they knew of the solemn moment at hand. The limousine driver and funeral director, Larry, opened the door and helped Abby exit the car. She could barely stand from the weight of grief. Her father, Mr. Miller gripped one arm and Larry held her other arm and escorted her to her seat. "My baby!!! Oh, my baby!" Abby wept aloud, resting her head on her Daddy's shoulders. The sound of Abby's cries were intense enough to bring the hardest heart of stone to tears.

The service was brief and consisted of a poem, Scripture, and remarks from Pastor Williams. It concluded with everyone singing, *"Jesus Loves Me."* My heart raced out of my chest as the time came for the final viewing and the closing of the tiny casket that would house Miguel until time was no more. I placed my hand over my heart in an attempt to decrease the rapid beating, but it was to no avail. I closed my eyes tightly and dropped my head as Larry entombed the casket and said, "Ashes to ashes, dust to dust."

There was a helpless feeling as Abby sat under the blue tent at the cemetery crying out to God for her baby. As I grieved with her, mourners and friends offered their condolences. I made sure to get at the back of the line, needing time to gather the right words to say. I wiped my sweaty palms on my black dress before extending it to Mr. Miller. "I'm so sorry," I patted his back. Then I knelt down on the faux lawn in front of Abby and held her as tightly as I could. "I love you and Miguel. He will always be in my heart," I whispered.

After a few seconds I pulled away to stand up, but Abby didn't loosen her grip. So I let her hold on to me until she was ready to let me go. I stood to my feet, kissed her wet, tear-stained cheek and headed to my car. Once in my car, I wondered where or how Abby found the strength to say goodbye to Miguel. From my perspective, that level of loss was the most difficult thing I had ever witnessed.

There was an enormous white cross in the middle of Baby Paradise. Something about that cross made me pause in my tracks. I immediately thought of Mary, the mother of Jesus and the pain she must have felt as she watched her son endure agony and ultimately death. I stared at the cross for several minutes before I could drive away from the cemetery. I said a simple prayer for Abby, asking God to give her the strength to carry her cross of suffering as she faced each coming day upon the painful road of grief.

Growing up I never knew pain. We lived well and enjoyed life. Being a happy, upper-middle class family, we were like the popular sitcom in the eighties. We took annual family vacations and participated in our church and community. My parents worked hard to provide for us. All our needs were met, but there were a few things we wanted and didn't get. Only a few instances of sickness can I recall within our family and even fewer deaths. My paternal great grandfather passed away when I was seven or eight years old. I still remember the night of his death. Our grandfather clock began to chime at a time other than directly on the hour. Soon afterwards the phone rang stating that "Pa-Pa" had passed away. At the time I didn't know what grief felt like and wouldn't be acquainted with grief for many years to come.

Each Thanksgiving my family would gather around my Grandma's table. We had a tradition of stating all of the things that we were thankful for before we shared a meal together. Most would thank the Lord that our circle had not been broken since the last time we gathered. It took me many years to understand what the saying really implied.

Chapter 3
Unplanned Pain

Being a fairly organized person, I enjoy planning events and celebrations. However, I don't like surprises. Rarely did I accept last minute invitations because they interfered with my prearranged plans. My favorite middle school teacher had a quote in her classroom that stated, "If you fail to plan – you plan to fail." That quote has resonated with me many times throughout my adult life. Now, I am not obsessive compulsive nor do I have to plan every single, minuscule detail, but I do have to plan.

My love for planning caused me to market myself as an event planner, specifically weddings, but I coordinated several birthday events as well. I am completely in my element when I can see a plan move from conception to fruition. Magic happens when an event comes alive. I liked the fact that everything moved at my command during an event. Planning every detail eliminated the chance for surprises.

When recounting my life, I planned every detail as much as possible: college, graduation from college, and finding the perfect job. I prayed for the perfect mate, which was as much planning as I could do in that regard. I dreamed of falling in love, but didn't actually have a plan for doing so. During my freshman year of high school, I had planned the first and middle names of each of my nine planned children. If I were going to have the nine kids, I suppose I would need a little assistance.

God sent a very unique gift my way packaged differently than I had ordered. I always knew I would be a mother and placed a great deal of thought in fulfilling my role. Somewhere in the recesses of my mind there was a husband who would genuinely love me and give me everything I ever wanted. I didn't know his name, but knew he'd be tall, with a fair complexion and handsome.

One Wednesday night after Bible study I met a short, handsome man, who introduced himself to me. "Hey, how are you? I'm Chris." he said as he extended his hand and smiled.

"Hey, I'm Tanika. Nice to meet you. Is this your first time here at the church?"

"Oh no, I've been here nearly every Sunday and Wednesday for the last seven months. I love it here."

In my mind I was thinking, *"Why is this guy talking to me?"* We made small talk for almost thirty minutes and exchanged numbers. In my brief encounter with him, I knew he was a good, respectful man. He even called me as we drove home from church. The conversation was great, although it could have easily been misinterpreted for a game of twenty questions. "What do you enjoy doing in your spare time? Do you travel much? Do you have any children?"

Each question was followed by a lengthy dialogue as we lost track of the time. He worked in the automotive industry but his real passion was broadcasting. The eligible bachelor had no kids and no baggage from previous relationships. He seemed to be a great catch and would likely make someone a very happy wife one day. By eleven o'clock, I knew I needed to conclude the call and prepare for bed. "Would it be okay if I gave you a call tomorrow, and perhaps we can grab some lunch after church on Sunday also?" he asked.

To my surprise, I consented to his request. I had never gone out with anyone from my church, nor had I given my number out for personal conversations. Since he wasn't my type I saw no harm in deviating from my plan, so for him, I found myself breaking my self-made rules. "Sure, you can give me a call tomorrow and I'll let you know about Sunday."

After a follow-up phone call on Thursday and lunch on Sunday, the rest is history. We communicated everyday and saw each other every weekend. We were just friends, but what a great friendship it was. He was such a nice guy: loving, compassionate, and embodying all of the qualities I wanted in a mate.

I "planned" to not allow myself to fall in love, for that would surely ruin the friendship that was now ten months old. It was a solid, safe friendship. There was no hand holding, no kissing, nothing except good conversation and quality time, and I was content with that. Chris, on the other hand, wanted more. "When can I get a real hug?" he asked one Sunday after a trip to the mountains.

"What do you mean by a real hug? Everyone gets the one arm hug and a few pats on the back from me – *everyone*," I emphasized.

Restraining from falling in love was my only sure way to detour the pain I had known. I didn't plan to have my heart broken and experience hurt from another failed relationship. Much to my surprise, I began to dream of building a life and a family with Chris. As much as I wanted to deny my feelings for my friend, my heart was drawn to him like bees to honey. Again my plan failed, and I was so glad it did. Little did I know my best days were ahead of me.

One Friday night we made a two hour drive up north to dine at Journey's, a new upscale restaurant. We laughed, sang, and danced in the car as if nothing or anyone else mattered. I eased my arm under his and smiled. He looked surprised and relieved that I initiated a sign that I wanted to be more than just his friend. *'This just feels right,'* I thought to myself.

We entered the crowded, dimly lit restaurant and had an extended wait time before being seated. Since it was a beautiful spring evening, we didn't mind passing the time in the courtyard of the restaurant. As we watched the sun set, Chris leaned in to kiss me on my cheek. Our eyes met as we smiled at the undeniable magic we felt between us.

The pager went off to signal that we were ready to be seated. We navigated through the crowd to our table and he pulled my chair out for me. We ordered our exquisite meal and enjoyed every morsel of it. As much as I appreciated the grand décor, the service, and the experience of Journey's, I was more elated to spend time with him.

The ride home was just as delightful as the trip to the restaurant. We sang along to classic love songs from the seventies and eighties. I did not want the night to end and certainly didn't want to disembark the love train we were on. Something about us being together just felt right.

At one o'clock in the morning, we arrived back at his house, physically tired, yet exhilarated by the experience we had. "Thank you so much for such a wonderful dinner date. I really enjoyed spending time with you," I said hugging his neck tightly.

Chris was taken aback by the lack of the one-armed hug he'd been accustomed to for the past ten months. "I'm glad you enjoyed yourself. I love being able to put a smile on your face," he said with a sheepish grin.

"Alright, I better get over to Lauren's house before it gets later. I'm staying over at her house tonight, and if I know her, she's waiting to hear all about our date," I said fumbling with my keys.

Chris gently lifted my chin and quickly pressed his soft lips against mine. We both laughed so loud we probably disturbed the neighbors. It was the perfect preschool type with two young, inexperienced lovers kissing for the first time. Perhaps laughter wasn't the correct response, but it certainly was the perfect way to conceal the nervousness we both felt. We didn't attempt a repeat kiss. After another hug that I initiated, I was off to Lauren's house. I put my car in reverse, grabbed my cell phone and pressed the number two to speed dial Lauren's mobile. "Hey, are you still up?"

"Of course, I'm up. How was it?" she asked.

I believe she could hear my smile through the phone as I swooned, "Wonderful, absolutely wonderful from beginning to end. I'm about three minutes from your house, so I'll fill you in when I get there."

"Okay, hurry up! I want to hear all about it!"

I drove in silent reflection as I replayed the events of the evening. I wouldn't have changed one single moment of our time together. My phone rang and I was jolted out of my daydream, but equally excited to see "Chris," appear on my caller ID. "Yes, Christopher?"

"I miss you already," he said softly.

"Oh, really? We've been together since five o'clock this afternoon and we've only been apart for less than five minutes?" I said sarcastically.

"I know and that's five minutes too long. I'm just going to marry you so I won't have to miss you like this again," he said with a sincere tone.

"You would marry me?"

"Yes, I would. You and I will, just wait and see. Are you at Lauren's house yet?"

"Okay I'm at the house," I laughed. "We will continue this discussion tomorrow."

When I turned the car off I watched the clouds seemingly dance around the moon. I couldn't help but imagine the possibilities of actually becoming his wife one day and hopefully soon. I wanted to jump out of my car at two o'clock in the morning and scream to all of the neighbors how much I loved him. Although, they probably wouldn't have appreciated my boisterous outburst. I knew Lauren was inside waiting to hear all about our date, so I used my key to her house and tried to be as quiet as possible. "Lauren, where are you?"

"Here I am!" she said and quickly walked out of her room.

"Why are you still wide awake?"

"I didn't want to go to sleep. I want to hear about your date. So, tell me everything."

Happily, I recounted the details of our evening together as if it were directly from the pages of a bestselling love story. I rambled on until three thirty in the morning. My love high had faded and sleep deprivation was in high gear. Lauren concluded the conversation with, "You have not stopped smiling since you walked in the door. I've never seen you this happy about anyone in all of the years I've known you. I can't wait to see where this goes."

Exactly one year to the date later, Chris took me out to dinner to celebrate our one-year dating anniversary. We were seated at a table facing the busiest street downtown. To my surprise there were a dozen beautiful, red, long stem roses waiting for me on our table. Even though I didn't like surprises, I was so impressed that he planned a surprise wedding proposal and even hired a photographer to capture the occasion. His vision was flawlessly executed. I even questioned him to see if he solicited Lauren's help but he didn't. At that moment our love for each other was evident to total strangers in the restaurant.

Chris and I planned every aspect of our wedding. Little did he know I had spent years watching *"The Life of a Wedding Planner"* and *"Baby Meets World."* I knew exactly what I wanted and purchased my wedding dress with our children in mind. I had to find a dress with an extended train, because I had a very unique plan. My train would be used to create the Christening gowns for my daughters. I was pretty certain that I'd have a few girls since I wanted a minimum of six kids. Initially I wanted nine, but one hot summer afternoon with my niece and nephew changed that.

After searching for the ultimate dress, I finally found the perfect designer dress in a catalog with an amazing Castilian train. I went to a local bridal shop to be fitted and without having ever laid my hands or eyes on the physical dress, I ordered it and wasn't concerned that I wouldn't like it – I just had to have it.

Without question, our wedding was everything I ever wanted and dreamed it would be. I had consumed quite a bit of wine on the eve of our big day and overslept for my eight am hair appointment, so my day started off later than I had planned. We had the perfect church that housed over five hundred guests. Our closest friends and family stood as attendants in the wedding. Talented singers and musicians provided musical selections like those of angels. The sound of the melodic tunes calmed my racing heart as I waited in the bridal chambers. I knew God's presence was with us on that beautiful October day. Surprisingly, Chris serenaded me as I entered the church. Oh my goodness, it was the best unplanned surprise ever!

We planned for a wonderful life together. We moved into our brand new home, just two months after our wedding. Everything was absolutely beautiful. We planned to love, to laugh and to give. We planned to have children and spoil their little behinds rotten. We never planned to say goodbye, especially not to our child – our children. We did not plan for pain.

Our wedding vows stated for better or for worse, but we only planned for better. The only pain I ever envisioned was the pain of childbirth, but I knew there would be planned pain medicine. Unfortunately, the pain we were introduced to did not come with an anesthetic, and to date there is no cure for this magnitude of pain. The pain of loss is incomparable to anything we have ever experienced. There was nothing to prepare us for goodbye, as we were only prepared to say hello.

Death unplanned, so sudden, so unfair, unplanned silence, unplanned tears, unanswered questions and unplanned fears.

Chapter 4
Happy Birthday!

For some reason I had been unusually emotional for a few days, but never gave much attention as to why. For the first time in seven years I grieved the loss of Grandma. I would often reflect on her advice *"To kill people with kindness,"* which was her way of telling me to take the high road if someone mistreated me. For the most part, I was able to slay giants because of her great wisdom. I also found myself chuckling at her quick wit and desire to *"whip somebody's backside with my cane,"* if they crossed her the wrong way. Though I never saw her beat anyone, I think the cane was reserved for anyone who had been killed one too many times with kindness, but didn't die.

In my emotions I thought of her with memories and smiles rather than tears. While standing in the hot shower on the eve of my birthday I cried as if it were that glorious August night on McCray Drive. I could feel her just as clearly as I felt the water upon my body. The smell of the fresh scent of her clothes on the clothesline allowed me to feel her presence blowing like a gentle breeze. "Hey Grandma! Oh, I sure have missed you," I said, looking around the shower with anticipation of seeing her. Tears lapped under my chin and my heart beat faster than the water falling from the shower head. The thought of being in her company once more was overwhelming. "I've dreamed of you so much. Are you okay?"

There was no response, although the power of her presence remained strong. "I have so much to…" I paused in the middle of my excitement, "…tell you." I felt like I just needed to be quiet. Perhaps I was speaking too loudly to hear Grandma's angelic voice. She didn't speak, so I waited, but never heard her voice. So, I stood against the wall of the shower, closed my eyes and mentally escaped to my favorite place…her lap. "I love you so much."

Minutes passed and there were still no words spoken, but clearly something was happening. I turned off the shower and sat on the toilet with hopes of an audible authentication of her presence. As the vapor from the steam-filled bathroom disappeared, so did her almost tangible presence. I remained in the bathroom for nearly an hour weeping.

When I woke up early Sunday morning, I decided the time had come to put my speculation to an end. My regular monthly guest, "Aunt Flo," was late for her predicted, always on time arrival date. The display window on the home pregnancy test read, "Positive." Immediately, I was moved to tears and my mind went fast forward. How would I break the news to Chris? I left him sleeping in our bedroom and eased into our office to create a card for him with the big news. I also had to calculate our due date, which took a few minutes longer than expected.

It was hard to think of the appropriate words to include in the card. I wanted it to be something creative and from the heart, but was racing against the clock. Chris would be waking up for church at any moment. I returned to our bedroom to find him already awake. So I slipped the card onto his side of the dresser and proceeded with my normal routine.

As he got dressed he picked up the card and said, "What's this?"

I grabbed the camera and waited for his reply. He looked at me with amazement and said, "Happy Father's Day? It's September. Father's Day is in June."

"Yes, daddy – Happy Father's Day."

Instantly, you could see the mental light come on. Chris was ecstatic. We hugged, laughed, and prayed for the special little miracle growing inside of me. Now I no longer wondered why Grandma visited me in the shower. She came to prepare my heart for the joy that was before us. How beautiful that my role model and inspiration of my dream of being a mother would visit me. She came as an angelic messenger to let me know that my dream had been fertilized into a growing reality. Just the Friday night before, there were twenty-nine candles on my birthday cake and little did I know twenty-nine thousand reasons to celebrate. I had a wedding rehearsal to conduct, so we had a late night birthday celebration at my favorite eatery downtown.

The next day we attended the Dickerson's wedding, had a visit from Grandma on Saturday, and found out we were expecting on Sunday. What an incredible weekend filled with my favorite things: good food, weddings, my favorite lady, and a baby! We made our way to church, but I can't recall much of the sermon. I kept thinking how we would announce our pregnancy to our family members.

My Mom called after her church service was over and asked if we were at home. She wanted to stop by for a few minutes to give me a birthday gift. Little did she know we had a gift for her as well. When she arrived, we chatted for a while, and I kept grinning, attempting to simmer the excitement bubbling within me. I asked her to guess what I got for my birthday. She thought jewelry, perhaps. After a few guesses, I gave her a Ziploc bag and said, "This is my birthday gift."

She looked at the pregnancy test in an inquisitive manner and then screamed as if she were the newest lottery winner. She wanted me to take her picture holding the positive test. She was wearing a royal blue suit, holding a test with a blue line, and absolutely positive that all signs were indicating that we were having a boy. Then she congratulated us and hugged us a million times. We had a full photo shoot with her holding my pregnancy test. She posed at the dining room table, in front of the fireplace, at the front door and at her car. I do believe she was excited.

Chris and I headed to my sister Tiffany's house to proclaim our new title as parents. Although I had planned for a creative way to share the news, I couldn't hold it in any longer. My sister was taking a Sunday afternoon nap when I eased beside her bed, nudged her and shoved the positive test in her face. Tiffany's sleep is more like hibernation; therefore, waking her from a state of relaxation usually yields a comical response. "Who?!" Tiffany replied.

I stood by her bed in silence and waited for the full message to translate in her brain. She transformed from a sleeping bear to an energized auntie right before my eyes. My nephew and two nieces wondered what all of the excitement was about and once we told them the news they were elated too.

Chris had a permanent smile on his face. Everyone knew he and I were in love with each other and already in love with our baby. The remainder of the afternoon and evening were spent calling our family to share the news. I called my GYN on Monday morning to report my pregnancy. They asked the date of my last menstrual cycle and told me my estimated due date. I was given an appointment for several weeks out.

The last call of the day was made to my cousin Maxine, who is an OB doctor in Virginia. She was elated to hear the news and asked all of the questions my doctor's office asked me. Meticulously reciting her mental check list, she advised me to take a prenatal vitamin with folic acid, eliminate caffeine, drink plenty of water, and listen to my body and rest when needed.

Fortunately for me I had no morning sickness and felt amazingly well. I already knew pregnancy would be a cakewalk for me. Chris and I shopped for maternity clothes, thought about nursery themes, baby names, maternity pictures, daycare, first day of school, graduations, wedding, grandchildren, and the lifetime we would have with this special baby.

I didn't want to tell my closest friends--who were more like sisters--the news over the phone. As fate would have it, we already had plans for a belated birthday dinner after work on Monday night. I was fairly certain I could hold the news for one more day, but I did spend the evening thinking of a way to tell them other than simply saying, "We're pregnant."

My heart raced as the six o'clock hour drew near. We all arrived at the Town Place Restaurant and were seated for our normal fun girl talk. The waitress took our drink orders and offered us a sample of wine. We ordered our entrées and continued our conversation, which was filled with a great deal of laughter and sharing memories of the past.

Tenille noticed that I hadn't touched my wine, so I offered it to her since I had no plans of even sampling it. After I passed the wine, I gave each of them an envelope. Dominique received a yellow envelope, Lauren received a pastel blue envelope and Tenille a pink one. Each of them gave me an inquisitive look and asked, "What is this Tee-Tee?"

The envelopes contained cards I made for each of them explaining how thankful I was we had shared so much through the years. I included pictures from previous birthday celebrations and outings of the four of us. Before they opened their envelopes, I grabbed the camera from my purse to capture the look on their faces as they read the last line of the card. *"We've shared so many fun times and now we will get to share the joy of raising a child together. Baby Dillard is coming May 2008."* Dominique immediately commenced to cry, which is par for the course for her. Tenille and Lauren were laughing, screaming, and crying simultaneously. "I knew it; I knew it Tee-Tee! That's why you didn't drink your wine," Tenille shouted.

Lauren's face turned red from her intense laughter and likely the wine also. Our waitress rushed over with our food and wanted to know what all the excitement was about and said, "I want to have some of whatever ya'll are having."

Tenille wiped tears from her face with the dinner napkin, pointed at me and said, "She's pregnant!!!"

The waitress congratulated me and quickly recanted her statement. She didn't want what we were having, but was happy to celebrate with us. I was pleased with how the surprise turned out. Although Dominique was the only one in the group who had a child, I knew they all would be vital in helping me navigate through the discovery of pregnancy.

My first appointment was nothing short of amazing. Chris and I sat patiently in the office with our handheld recorder. I recall the look of indescribable, undeniable amazement on Chris's face as we heard the sound of our baby's heartbeat for the first time. We saw a tiny, active baby on the ultrasound – everything was perfect. After that appointment they scheduled me to return in six weeks for a gender ultrasound. Not a minute or day passed when we didn't think of how much our lives would change and how we would absolutely lavish every ounce of love we had for each other on our precious baby. What an incredible journey we had embarked upon. Indeed, it was the best of times!

When the Thanksgiving holiday came I was so excited to spend my favorite holiday with my family. I was also elated to show off my new baby bump and maternity outfits. Without a question, we had so much to be thankful for. When our turn came to recount our blessings prior to the meal, we thanked God for many things but most importantly, for blessing us with a baby. My pregnancy progressed flawlessly. I looked fabulous; I felt amazing, and I was the happiest pregnant woman I knew.

Chapter 5
I Can't Dismiss This Feeling

We wanted to decorate our home for the holidays before the hustle and bustle of the season started. Looking through the weekly circulars, I complained about our tiny branch of a Christmas tree that fit perfectly in our old one bedroom apartment, but our new house needed a new bigger (*much bigger*) tree.

Thursday evening, Chris came home from work a bit later than usual. I was not keenly aware of the time as I came directly in the house, planted myself on the couch and fell fast asleep. As much as I hated surprises, he again surprised me with a 12-foot pre-lit Christmas tree. Little did he know it was the exact tree I wanted.

When I was growing up, I don't remember having a Christmas tree up during the first week of December. Our tree was beautiful and was the perfect fit for our home. After we decorated the tree, Chris and I cuddled on the sofa and talked about how our next Christmas would have pink or blue ornaments and a ton of presents for our new baby. The best of times were before us, and our future was as bright as the lights that were shining from our Christmas tree.

As I prepared for bed on December 4, 2007 there was this unshakeable, unsettling feeling. I looked at my reflection in the bathroom mirror, *'God, something is going on and I feel it.'* I went to bed and slept peacefully until my house phone rang shortly after 5am. No one ever calls our home this early unless there is bad news. When I answered the phone my aunt's voice trembled as she informed me that my daddy had fainted at his home and had been taken to the emergency room at the local hospital.

While she was talking I couldn't gather my thoughts enough to move any faster than a slug. I woke Chris and told him about the call and my eerie thoughts from the night before. *'Surely, this had to be exactly what I sensed last night,'* I thought.

Chris had to remind me of the scripture in Isaiah 43:1-2:

But now, this is what the LORD says--he who created you, O Jacob, he who formed you, O Israel: "Fear not, for I have redeemed you; I have summoned you by name; you are mine. When you pass through the waters, I will be with you; and when you pass through the rivers, they will not sweep over you. When you walk through the fire, you will not be burned; the flames will not set you ablaze.

Clearly the Lord had prepared both of our hearts for the unfolding event, and we had the instruction from Him to fear not. I'm thankful for the spiritual connection Chris and I share with each other and in our relationship with God.

I arrived at the emergency room and found my Daddy resting comfortably. Several tests were performed and our family waited for the results in the waiting area. In truth, we were all silently nervous, but the conversation revolved around my baby bump and pregnancy to mask our anxiety. I made several trips to the restroom in a very short period of time, but during one of those trips I felt a sudden pain in my abdomen. Of course, I assumed the baby felt my anxiety and was perhaps in an uncomfortable position, so when the pain quickly resolved, I made my way out of the restroom just in time to hear we could visit Daddy.

All of the test results came back normal and his fainting episode likely occurred due to low blood pressure. What a relief! Daddy is extremely modest and has an impeccable work ethic. He wanted to know why we all were there at the hospital and not at our jobs. After he said that, I knew Daddy was okay.

The next day I headed to work and released words of thanksgiving to God and happy tears. Despite the happy ending to the climactic event, I still had an inkling of uneasiness with me, but still couldn't quite identify the origin. My workday was normal; however, I was mentally and emotionally exhausted. I just wanted to go home for an afternoon nap.

I started to pack my belongings but needed to visit the ladies' room. I returned to my desk to complete my task of packing up and needed to make another trip to the ladies' room. It was clear to me I had drunk an excess of my 64 ounces of water for the day, and my bladder just couldn't hold fluid like it used to. *'Welcome to the real world of pregnancy,'* I thought.

Finally, I was ready to leave for the day but sat down to answer a quick phone call. When I stood up I felt warm fluid running down my leg. My little baby was sitting on my bladder for sure. I did a speed walk to the restroom but the more I walked the more fluid came. I couldn't stop the flow no matter how much I tried to grip my kegel muscles. I managed to sit on the toilet just in time to hear what sounded like a rubber band being popped. The popping sound was followed by an extreme gush of fluid.

My heart pounded out of my chest. What was happening to me and more importantly to my baby? I ripped off my black maternity pants and smelled them to make sure it was urine and not blood. There was absolutely no scent. The water in the toilet was cloudy and slightly the color of brass or wheat. I was pretty certain it wasn't urine, but what it actually was remained a mystery.

Beads of sweat lined my face like pearls as I gathered myself to return to my office. Immediately, I pulled out my cell phone and called my OB's office. It was the end of the day and I didn't want to bother them, but I wasn't sure what to do. Thankfully, Anne, the nurse, answered the phone. I told her I was sixteen weeks pregnant. I recalled what I had experienced and asked her what to do next. Anne agreed the baby was likely on my bladder and instructed me to go home, rest for the night and call the office again if I experienced any more gushes of fluid.

After talking to her there was an immediate feeling of relief but also one of anxiety in the same moment; then I called my momma. She bore three children, so she should know something. Even if she didn't know exactly what I was experiencing, she'd be able to say something to reassure me. When my mother answered the phone, she could tell by the trembling in my voice that something was wrong. "Momma, I think my water just broke," I said holding back my tears.

As I told her the story, I could hear the anxiety in her voice. "Where are you? Have you called Chris? Have you called the doctor? Did you call Maxine?"

I answered all of her questions as the tears flowed freely. "You are really early for your water to break, but you are going to be okay. We just have to trust God," she said in a comforting voice.

When I looked at the clock, it was 5:25p.m. and I was still sitting in the parking lot. Chris called me every day as soon as he got off work and that day was no different. My phone rang and I blurted out the story. He laughed and interjected, "Babe, you just peed on yourself." In his laughter I found nothing funny and continued my story in tears. I was scared and aggravated because he didn't know how serious this event was.

Slowly, I reclined my seat and drove home silently praying my baby was alright. When I got home I plopped on the couch, elevated my feet and watched the lights on our beautiful Christmas tree. Chris came into the quiet house and when he saw me on the couch he knelt down beside me, kissed my forehead, and started wiping my tears. He really couldn't comprehend the magnitude of what was going on, but seeing my emotional state made him aware of the possibility of heartbreak.

The thoughts in my head were numerous. I wanted to remain positive, but for every good thought, there were ten "what ifs." I was exhausted, desperately needing physical and mental rest. Chris and I prayed the good Lord would hear and honor our prayers. After all, we are good people and didn't deserve any undue trials in our lives. All night I tossed and turned, having a series of dreams in between my sleep/wake cycles. One of the dreams was filled with beautiful music. There was magnificent choir singing a song I had never heard before. Despite the heavenly serenade, restlessness overcame me, and I longed for the light of a new day.

Morning came and I clung to a positive attitude and hoped for the best news. Everything seemed normal, and there was no blood, no pain. Most importantly, there were no more sudden gushes of fluid. *'We're safe,'* I thought. I continued to hear the song from my dream echo in my ear, so I penned the chorus of the song on paper.

After writing down the words to the song, I made my way to work and progressed through the day as if the prior day had never even happened. I never spoke a word about the events to my officemate or other co-workers. I did however call my cousin Maxine and left a voicemail message asking her to call me back.

Maxine returned my call with no delay and I went into another office to explain my story to her. During our conversation there were periods of silence, which caused my heart to pound. I wanted to hear interjections of, "Oh, that's okay. Yes, that's normal," or "You are going to be fine." In a matter of minutes my first cousin became my primary OB, and took me on as a new patient.

Maxine was calm, but firmly encouraged me to go to the emergency room. She didn't give any statistics, but strongly suggested I be observed and placed on antibiotics without delay. Surprisingly, the focus was totally on me and not the baby. She asked me about twenty times if I wanted her to come to South Carolina. Instantly, I knew I wasn't in the safety zone I expected.

Immediately after speaking with Maxine, I called my OB and was instructed to come into his office the following day. Just as I was preparing to leave work, Chris called to report that his sister Jaye was being admitted to the hospital for an emergency C-section. Her twenty-seven-week old twins were being delivered early due to preeclampsia. "Can you head over to the hospital to be with her?" he asked.

Without question, I agreed to go. I couldn't imagine facing an emergency C-section alone. So I rushed to the hospital just in time to try to calm her before the procedure. I exchanged my brown polka dot maternity shirt for blue scrubs and said a prayer with Jaye as she was wheeled to the operating room. There I was instructed to wait outside until the epidural had been administered. After what seemed like forever, I was permitted into the freezing cold operating room.

The look on Jaye's face proved how scared she was. All I could do was reassure her that everything was going to be fine and she'd see the kids in a few brief moments. Shortly thereafter, Baby Girl A, entered the world weighing 1 lb 8 oz, followed by Baby Boy B who entered the world weighing 1 lb 3oz. The smallest little miracles had arrived!!!

My heart leaped with joy to witness such an extraordinary event. The babies were taken to the NICU after we were able to glance at them for five seconds. While Jaye was resting I went to share the good news with the family. The twins were small, but they were very healthy. However, they would have to remain in the NICU for several months before being allowed to come home. After a long, adventurous evening we headed home to retire for the night. Unfortunately, I had a hard time falling asleep, reminiscing about the beauty of the twins' birth and the pain Jaye felt when she had to be separated from them. Despite the early, unplanned induction and necessary separation, we were thankful everything was well.

By the time I returned home, I was exhausted and needed a shower. Maxine had left a message asking about my condition, but there was nothing to report. Taking the easy approach, I sent a quick text message. "I will call you after my appointment in the morning." As instructed, we arrived at our appointment the following day. Although, we heard a heartbeat with the handheld Doppler, Dr. Laurel wanted a more detailed ultrasound, so he sent me to the hospital. He couldn't confirm or give much detail about my fluid until the ultrasound was completed. Hearing the baby's heartbeat gave a sense of peace.

Chris had an appointment scheduled for his back the same time I was due for the ultrasound and wanted to cancel. I insisted he go and promised to call him as soon as the sonogram was over, or he could just come to the hospital to wait for me if I had not contacted him. Though he was reluctant, he obliged. My heart raced out of my chest as I sat in the exam room. The sonographer came in, started the procedure and pointed out the features of the baby. When I saw our little baby moving about, I was relieved.

The sonographer became very quiet and turned the screen away from me. "Is everything okay?"

"I'm not able to tell you anything right now. You'll need to wait for the doctor. I'm going to step out to call him now," she replied.

There was complete silence in the room except for the pounding of my heart. Her comment caused my momentary relief to escalate into sheer panic. My hands were shaking, and beads of sweat poured down my neck. I reached for my cell phone to call Maxine, but had to leave a message. "Max, something is wrong. I just had the ultrasound, but the tech turned the screen away from me and left to call my doctor. She won't tell me anything. Please call me as soon as you can."

Within three minutes the tech came back and gave me the telephone. It was my doctor. "Tanika, the ultrasound shows that you have no amniotic fluid. This condition is called Premature Rupture of Membranes (PROM). We are admitting you, so we can start IV antibiotics to prevent infection." He cleared his throat and briefly paused. "Chances of life without amniotic fluid are nearly impossible at this gestational age. The fluid is necessary for the lungs to grow and develop. Unfortunately, the chances that the amniotic sac will re-seal are practically impossible – I'm sorry."

"Is there anything that can be done to save the pregnancy--anything?" I asked. Our options were miniscule and he reiterated that starting the IV antibiotics would be in our best interest. It was the worst of times. Did I hear Dr. Laurel's report accurately? Surely, we were not facing this magnitude of a crisis.

Immediately, I felt like I had shattered into a million pieces. Our hopes, dreams, and plans for the future were soon to come to a certain end. I walked through the haze-filled room, found my cell phone to make the call to Chris. "Babe, where are you?"

Hearing the despair and anxiety in my voice, he said he was almost at the hospital. I tried to explain the enormous valley of pain that was before us, but I couldn't give him that kind of news over the phone. I needed him and he needed me. Within minutes Chris was hurriedly escorted to the exam room where he found me openly sobbing. With magnetic force, my head was pinned to his chest and the weeping intensified. The pain was too great to verbalize. "So, it really was your water that broke?" I slowly nodded in the affirmative. "What do we do now?"

"No," I said slightly raising my head from his chest.

The sonographer returned to the room with a wheelchair and explained her findings, then echoed Dr. Laurel's instructions. We were not prepared at all for what we were about to embark upon. They wheeled me out of the exam room, down an endless corridor and into a black elevator. I held my head down for the duration of the transport and shielded my face with my right hand as Chris held my left hand.

The elevator doors opened to the 4th floor, the Labor and Delivery Unit, which would be my home for the next few days. My eyes were fixated upon the black and ivory tile pattern on the floor. Our three team caravan stopped at the nurse's desk to give a report and obtain my room assignment. I never looked up or moved my hand from my face – I could only cry. The tears gathered at my chin and dripped down my chest. "It's okay, Babe – it's okay," Chris said holding my hand a little tighter. I never had a reason in the past to doubt Chris's words, but I couldn't see that anything was going to be okay.

We settled into the room and I was able to give my account of Dr. Laurel's instructions. We called, emailed and sent text messages to our family members, church members, coworkers, and friends and urged for their immediate, unrelenting prayers for a miracle. Lauren, Dominique, and Tenille responded immediately. I couldn't compose myself enough to talk on the phone, so I resorted to text messaging only.

Tenille's office was a stone's throw away from the hospital. She sent a text stating that she was on her way, but I told her not to come. They had all seen the good, bad, and ugly side of me through the years, but this time was different. I didn't want them to see me in such a broken, fragile, and emotional state. It was also important for me to protect Chris's emotions.

Dr. Halton, a very handsome, blue-eyed Maternal Fetal Medicine specialist made rounds in our room early that afternoon. He introduced himself to Chris and me and informed us that he works very closely with Dr. Laurel and that he wanted to do another ultrasound. He wanted to see the condition of the baby, my amniotic sac and fluid for himself. During the procedure he was quiet and released a few heavy sighs. He confirmed that I had virtually no amniotic fluid and the chances of the sac resealing were slim, but possible.

Before we had a chance to respond, he proclaimed he was a man of faith and despite his professional judgments he believed in God and the miracles that He can perform. Dr. Halton admonished us to call everyone of faith we knew to pray with us for a better outcome. For the first time since receiving the devastating news, I saw a flicker of hope and heard something other than despair. Chris and I looked at each other and smiled. *'If all of the people we know bombard heaven, we really are going to be okay,'* I thought.

During my two-day hospital stay I still wondered why in the world this was happening to us. I was instructed to go home, drink plenty of water. My activity level was listed as strict bed rest. I saw my OB weekly, but spent most of my days lying on my back and occasionally moving to the recliner for a change of scenery. I prayed over our precious baby and sang songs of victory over him/her. Each day inside of my womb was another day closer to an increased chance of survival.

At the first weekly visit, we heard a very strong heartbeat and saw movement on the ultrasound. Maybe things were really going to be okay. Dr. Laurel, Anne, and the other nurses were surprised at our baby's viability despite being in a fluidless sac. We saw hope and the prayers for a miracle being answered. We left the office feeling encouraged and were eager to return the next week to see our baby continue to thrive and defy the odds. We were equally excited to have the long anticipated anatomy scan to reveal the gender.

Our second week at home was much like the first: bed rest, recliner rest, sleep, dream, pray, eat, repeat. My dreams were vivid and more intense. I recall hearing other expectant mothers say they had incredibly wild dreams during pregnancy, so I assumed my dreams were par for the course – or were they? I kept a journal beside my bed, because I would awake from a dream and hear a celestial choir sing amazing songs I've never heard before. Quickly, I'd scribble the words down using my cell phone for light and drift back off to sleep.

There were mornings I grabbed the journal to show Chris the words to a song, but the paper would be a blank slate. I didn't realize I dreamed that I wrote the words down. As I explained the dream to Chris, I'd try to recapture the melody in my heart. For some reason I had the greatest peace when I had those dreams. I knew I was in the presence of God, and He was providing me the strength I needed to face these uncertain times. Every day I'd shared each experience with Chris so he could receive the same peace and encouragement that had been given to me.

One Sunday night I drifted off to sleep and was in a white, sterile room preparing for delivery. Chris was standing by my side rubbing my forehead when I felt the severe pain of labor, but I did not utter a word. My head and hands were sweaty, my heart pounded and the pain was no more. I looked between my legs and there was a baby exiting my womb. Seemingly, with all of my strength gone I whispered, "Give it to the Father." Chris's hand remained on my head and two hands were positioned to receive our baby.

My eyes opened from the dream, and I wondered what the Lord was saying to me. I could not wait for Chris to wake up; he had to hear the dream and interpret it for me. "Babe, what do you think that means?" I asked.

"I don't know," he said shaking his head.

We both knew but confessing this truth was an insurmountable task. The dream troubled me and gave me peace at the same time. All I could do was- sit in my recliner and pray. My prayer of declaration turned into a song to remind me that God was strong, mighty, and able. I grabbed my laptop and wrote out the chorus of the song and then the verses. Chris brought me the handheld recorder so I could record the song. I knew I would need to be reminded of this truth in the days to come.

On December 18th my momma came over to spend the evening with me. Chris had gone to be with one of our friends who had lost his mother unexpectedly that day. I migrated from the couch to the recliner trying to find the perfect comfortable place. I made a trip to the guest bathroom and noticed some spotting in my underwear. I wiped again and again, but each time I saw pink and then eventually a bright red blood. My mind was consumed with thoughts of what could be going on inside of my body. I wanted to tell Momma right away, but didn't want to sound an alarm and pull Chris away from our grieving friend. So, I decided to keep quiet until Chris came home. In the meantime, I elevated my feet and drank plenty of water.

The clock ticked at a snail's pace. The few hours that Chris was gone seemed like an eternity. He called as he was making the forty-five-minute drive home. "Is everything okay, babe?"

"Yeah, I'm okay, just hurry home," I lied. I couldn't give him bad news over the phone.

There was a pause on the other end of the phone. Then he asked, "Are you sure you're okay?"

"I'm fine, really. Just hurry home to us," I laughed subtly to mask the lump of tears in my throat. To keep him from panicking I quickly changed the subject and asked how our friends were doing. After getting Chris off the phone I positioned myself on the couch and placed my head away from view to hide my tears from Momma. I knew if I started crying with her, I wouldn't stop. She offered to make dinner and her offer could not have come at a more opportune time.

Momma was in the kitchen preparing one of my favorite pregnancy cravings, Cajun shrimp pasta, as I sat on the couch riding the waves of my tears. In what seemed like a flash, I heard Chris's truck enter the driveway and the engine shut off. I did not have a plan as to how to tell him things were not fine as I declared. Chris came in the house and greeted Momma in the kitchen and knelt beside me on the couch in the living room. When my eyes met his he knew something wasn't right. "What's wrong?"

"Nothing," I just shook my head.

"Well, why are you crying?"

"Something is wrong. I went to the bathroom earlier and there was some kind of thick mucus, I had spotting in my underwear, and saw bright red blood when I wiped. I don't think this is a good sign."

Chris sighed heavily and closed his eyes. "Did you call Dr. Laurel?"

I explained why I didn't call the doctor and why I did not tell Momma. Momma had come into the room with us. I had to tell her everything. She and Chris thought I should get in bed and try to relax. I complied and called the on-call pager for Dr. Laurel. Within minutes he returned the call and I gave him a detailed description of everything. They instructed me to come in at 9 a.m., the next day to be checked. Of course, Dr. Laurel told me that if the pain increased or if I soaked a pad in an hour or less to head straight to the hospital. Momma prayed with us before she left and told us that everything would be alright. I didn't sleep at all. Chris tossed and turned all night. I made several trips to bathroom during the early morning hours and to my surprise, there was no more blood.

The next morning we arrived early to our appointment as we were anxious for some hopeful news. When the nurse used the Doppler and didn't find a heartbeat, she immediately left the room and came back with the ultrasound machine and Dr. Laurel. The silence in the room was suffocating. Our worst nightmare had become a reality – our baby had no heartbeat. It was the winter of despair!

Chapter 6
After Life

Again we were admitted in the hospital. They placed me in room 439 for an induction. The minutes seemed like days as we awaited the arrival of our baby. My nurse Kim spent a great deal of time with us as we completed the necessary paper work. She also encouraged us to make decisions about arrangements. "What is the normal thing to do for a nearly nineteen week old baby," we pondered.

My momma was right by our side for the process to offer support and suggestions. Her cell phone rang constantly as news of our despair spread to our family and church members. Momma had the task of being the messenger. There was no way we could bring ourselves to speak of our painful loss. Thank goodness she was buckled in for the ride and had no plans for leaving us.

The only person I spoke with was Maxine. She was my lifeline – I didn't have to be strong for her. Maxine was familiar with neonatal demise. She had witnessed more than her share of painful, premature hellos and unwanted, heartbreaking goodbyes. Maxine verbally walked me through a crash course of *"What to Anticipate When Expecting Death."*

"Tee, how much do you want to know?" she inquired passionately.

"Tell me everything; I don't want to be surprised."

Maxine just had a way with her words. More than eight hours and hundreds of miles away, she seemed to be seated beside me in room 439. "Tee, I'm here if you need me. Do you want me to catch a flight and come to the hospital?" I knew she meant every word, but I reassured her that she should be at home with her two-year-old son and husband. Besides, it was just a few days before Christmas.

Dr. Laurel explained how the process of induction would work. I signed consent for the medication and he inserted two small white pills onto my cervix. The pills would prepare my body for labor. He informed us that process could take several hours. The good news was that I wouldn't have to fully dilate, since the baby was so small. After four hours of labor, I was dilated enough to deliver. Dr. Laurel adjusted my bed and positioned my legs and feet for delivery. He sat at the end of the bed and coached me into taking slow, deep breaths. I held onto Chris's hand in an effort to minimize the pain. I was too afraid to speak. "Are you ok?" Chris asked in a caring tone as he gripped my hand.

My husband and I nodded in the affirmative. After two to three minimal pushes our baby entered the world silently on December 19, 2007 at eighteen weeks, four days weighing 7 oz and was seven inches long. I cannot recall a time in my life when I had been so afraid. As prepared as I thought I was to meet our baby, the reality of the actual event proved otherwise. A myriad of emotions crippled me. I was angry that our innocent child suffered without a cause for weeks and endured one final wound during the birthing process. My body failed our child – the place that should have been the safest place ended up being the deadliest.

There was so much uncertainty as to how to face the coming days. The thought of continuing life without our baby seemed unfair. I felt like I was robbed of our hopes, dreams, and desires to have a family. *'Why had our prayers not been heard?'* I wondered. There was an equal amount of pain and pride in the same moment. I was proud of what our love had produced; however, I was pained that our love for God and each other was not enough to keep our child with us.

Despite our best efforts, we could not identify the anatomy of the baby. We would have to wait for genetic results from the pathology lab to put our speculations to rest. Baby Dillard, was perfect in every way, just born too soon because of my imperfect body. We held our child, loved "it" and wished that our present fate was not reality. Without question, I gave birth to a strong little fighter. Chris, Momma, and I spent hours holding Baby Dillard's fragile body. We sang to our beloved child and filled a few hours with a lifetime of love. We wanted to see every detail in an attempt to determine who the baby would have looked like.

Our time with Baby Dillard was much too brief and the memories far too few. As we decided to rest our weary bodies for the night, the head nurse came and took Baby Dillard to the morgue. A hospital blanket was draped over an emesis basin carrying our tiny baby. Our final goodbye had just occurred. There was no beauty in our baby's death or our farewell.

My grief was profound. It transcended all reason and gripped the very core of my being. I left the hospital empty with an empty memory box, empty arms, empty womb, empty photo album and empty emotions. I felt helpless and equally powerless, having nothing to show for a life that once was.

We opted against having a funeral service. The thought of placing such a tiny frame in the ground and heaping mounds of dirt upon it seemed so unshakably disturbing. I cringed at the thought of Chris and I tiptoeing through a graveyard to place flowers upon our child's grave on holidays or birthday. The mere thought of standing over our child's grave seemed unnatural.

Chris and I received great love and support from our family and friends, but nothing would change the fact that our firstborn was no longer with us. There were countless nights of sobbing and everything reminded me of what we did not have. I found solace sitting in my quiet home, curtains drawn, staring into the pictures of my imagination. How I longed to know the feeling of a fetal kick or turn inside of me, but there was only hollowness. How I craved the discomfort of pregnancy, which I would have gladly traded for the distress in my heart.

During our grief I also wanted to know the depth of the pain in Chris' head and heart. The pain was insurmountable for him and he found that withholding his emotions both verbally and emotionally was what he needed to do in order to be strong for me. I watched him bottle his pain and make honest strides to return to life before loss. I wanted to move forward and be happy again, but pain was ever before me. There were so many unanswered questions about the past that made the forecast for my future questionable.

I looked forward to my post-partum six-week follow up appointment with excitement and trepidation. I wanted answers as to why this tragedy ever happened, when we could try to conceive again and most importantly, the sex of our baby. It was important for me to have an identity for our baby. I no longer wanted to call our baby an "it/him or her." I wanted to see our baby in our dreams in either a pink dress with frills and bows or our son with a baseball cap and "lil' slugger" outfit. We needed clarity and the revealing of the missing puzzle piece.

Our hearts felt the heaviness of returning to the place where we heard our child's heartbeat for the first time and saw vibrant movement on ultrasound. We had memories of the past and only medical records in the present. Dr. Laurel was very gentle in his medical approach. He asked how we were doing, expressed his condolence again and encouraged us to seek a support group or counsel through our church if we felt we needed to talk. He examined me and found that my body was healing nicely. He reviewed my laboratory results and thankfully there were no signs of infection that attributed to my water breaking prematurely. He then reviewed the pathology reports and found that there were no abnormalities with our child. All forty six chromosomes were present without defect. We were delighted to hear that we could resume our quest to build a family in March, which was three months post delivery.

Unfortunately, Dr. Laurel could not provide a definitive answer as to why our child's demise occurred. Medically, everything was slated for a perfect pregnancy. We were told that miscarriages were common for the first pregnancy and that many women go on to have healthy, full term pregnancies after loss. There is often no medical or scientific evidence to support a fetal loss; sometimes this just happens. Although we did not have concrete answers, we were comforted to know there was nothing wrong with us or our baby. He also informed us that trying again should yield more favorable results.

"Do either of you have any questions for me?" Dr. Laurel asked with a smile before telling us that he wouldn't have to see us again until we were pregnant.

Chris and I looked at each other with raised brows as if to imply who would be the one to ask "the" question. "Yes, we have one question," I asked. "Were you able to tell the sex of the baby?"

"Yes, it was a girl," he replied.

Chris sighed loudly and I smiled as the tears flowed simultaneously. I immediately envisioned our daughter in her daddy's arms. I saw our princess in her dedication gown made from the train of my wedding dress. "I will make a copy of the pathology report to give to you. Get dressed and I will meet you out front," he instructed.

Dr. Laurel gave us the pathology reports and wished us the best. I held on to those two sheets of paper for dear life. Aside from our memories and mental pictures, a pathology report was all that we had to prove that our baby girl ever existed. Chris and I prepared to leave the office but spent several minutes in the parking lot conversing about our visit. While we were talking he received a call from his momma to say that his sister was on the way home from the NICU with her daughter.

Of course, Chris said that he would be right over. This would be the first time that he would see his little miracle of a niece in person. He had that look of excitement that I had visualized he would have when he held our daughter. The thought of actually traveling with him for such a joyous homecoming caused the gaping fissure in my heart to enlarge instantly. "Do you want to go?" he asked.

"No, you can go ahead. I will see her later," I said in an attempt to swallow the lump in my throat.

I drove home slowly with tears in my eyes and the pathology reports in my lap. Life was so very unfair, especially at that moment. I had to hold it together until I made it to the safety of my home. All of the strength I had was exhausted as I crawled into bed and broke into pieces. Our attempt to build a family had broken my heart.

Chapter 7
Dream Again

Chris and I desperately needed to emotionally turn the page of grief. Our life had been dark, dull, and downright painful. Six weeks after our loss I returned to work. There was an enormous black cloud that seemed to hover over me. Shame and embarrassment engulfed me. There was nothing to show for the life that was such a large part of my heart. I didn't want sympathy; I wanted to be alone. I did not want the sad looks and I definitely didn't want to answer questions. I did not care to assist people in removing their foot from their mouths after they realized their statements were inappropriate. I did not want my co-workers to see me cry. I just wanted to get away from it all – permanently.

Every day, I drove home from work in absolute silence and occasionally considered which light post to wrap my red coupe sports car around. I longed for my baby. I had to be her mother, even if it meant forcing my way into heaven to see her again. While I was at work I didn't speak to anyone about my emotions and suicidal ideations. My emotions were off-kilter and far from the normal stages of grief based on everything I had read.

Most of my longing for isolation stemmed from all of the happiness that engulfed our office. I was the thirteenth employee in my office to be expecting a baby that year. The buzz was always that someone had just found out they were having a girl. Another employee was adopting a boy, someone else had just delivered a baby and another woman was returning from maternity leave. Good news was all around me and there was no escaping the black cloud that threatened everyone else's happiness. So I resolved to stay in my office, unless I had to go to the restroom. I further resolved to eat lunch at my desk or in my car so I could have a few moments to myself without having to be happy for anyone or face the uneasy quietness that filled a room whenever I entered.

In large, people (co-workers, church members, family, and friends) did not know what to say. The most appreciated words were simply, "I'm sorry, you're in my prayers." We heard many reasons and religious explanations as to why God took our baby and not a single one of them made sense to me. My blood pressure escalated as people made comments like: "Maybe you just weren't ready to be a mom. Maybe the baby had something wrong with her and God decided to take her. Maybe you just tried to do too much while you were pregnant. Maybe God needed another flower in His garden. You guys are young; God will just give you another baby."

Perhaps any of these suggested verdicts could have been the case, but I wanted to assemble a couple of profane words together and defend myself by simply saying, "It was not my fault. I wanted our baby, even if she was not perfect by the standards of others!" However, it was easier to keep silent, smile, and thank them for their well intended, yet offensive comments.

Isolation and depression had to be evicted from my thoughts and our home. Chris and I had to dream again! We had to find a hope that was greater than our pain. There was no twelve-step program or medication that would change our situation. We simply made the choice to believe that God really did love us and despite one catastrophic event, we were going to maintain our faith, hope, and trust in Him, and felt confident that trusting Him again wouldn't be a bad idea. We had to be at peace, knowing that our questions could never be answered until we saw Jesus face to face.

Seemingly, pain had been assigned to us, but it certainly was not going to define us. So we decided to return to church and get back involved in our active leadership roles. I cried and sang when I needed an avenue to release the pain and reflected on the pregnancy to fuel my dreams. Chris was so strong. I never saw him cry. He was never discouraged. After all, everyone said, "Be strong for Tanika." And that is exactly what he did. Chris suppressed his emotions by keeping busy, but several nights of pillow talk and shared prayers let me know that he was hurting. However, he was committed to taking care of me and not the reverse.

In February, I had a business trip to San Diego. It had been scheduled since October, during my first trimester of pregnancy. After our pregnancy loss, the trip proved to be the perfect escape. Chris came with me and it was just what we needed. We were out in public and no one looked at us with an eye of pity. No one rubbed our backs and offered condolences. No one knew our names or our story and that's just the way we wanted it.

I attended my required sessions by day while Chris toured the city. In the afternoons and evenings we would sit by the pier and share our dreams for the future with our babies, growing old together and traveling the world. For the first time in months I heard Chris laugh. I saw his gentle smile and true happiness illuminate his eyes. It was like we had to go across the country just to dream again. Finally, we were happy and free! The trip helped navigate our emotional course.

We both had vibrant dreams about our growing family. I dreamed of a newborn baby, while Chris dreamed of a family portrait with two beautiful little girls dressed in white. I wanted as much detail from Chris as possible. I specifically wondered if the girls were wearing white dresses made from my wedding train. Did they have my dimples and Chris's gentle nature? Not only were we dreaming, but other people were sharing in our dreams. Several people said they had a prophetic insight and saw us with a baby.

We watched the calendar closely and recounted Dr. Laurel's instructions for when it was safe to try to conceive again. March had finally arrived!!! We were diligent about planning and tracking cycle and ovulation days. We did not want to prolong the expansion of our family any longer. We had dreamed of it for much too long. Reality had to come.

April 8th was the anniversary of our dating courtship and our engagement. It was also the day I noticed my cycle had not arrived. I tested at four o'clock in the morning. The anxiety was killing me. As fate would have it, the pregnancy test was positive!!! We were expecting our love child, whom we conceived in March. *'Ahhh, I just love it when a plan comes together!'*

We did not hesitate to tell our family! We were the proud heralds of the news. By seven o'clock that morning, we had called our mothers and shared the information. My calculated due date was December 28th. *'Another December baby,'* I thought. We were so overjoyed at our wonderful blessing being knitted in my womb. "Everything is sure to work out this time," I assured myself and others.

Dr. Laurel immediately called me in for lab work. The results were perfectly normal, except for my progesterone level. He gave me a prescription for the medicine to strengthen my cervix. I took the medicine as prescribed and we proceeded with optimism and faith.

When we got home there was a tiny package in the mail from our godparents, Momma and Pop Dawkins. Inside the package was a small Baby's First Bible. Momma Dawkins neatly inscribed beautiful words from her heart into the cover of the book. "Dear Baby, Grandpa Dave and I are so excited about your arrival. We pray for you daily. Here is our first of many gifts to you. Hide this word in your heart. We love you! Nammy and Poppie Dawkins."

We quickly started planning the nursery, the perfect name, maternity photos, baby showers, baby dedications, first birthday, graduation, wedding, growing old and becoming grandparents. Everything before us – everything. As my pregnancy progressed flawlessly, I looked fabulous, I felt amazing, and I was the happiest pregnant woman I knew.

The first trimester came and went with no problem. However, I was seen frequently by both my regular OB and my high-risk OB. We went to see Dr. Halton on Thursday, July 17th for a cervical check and gender ultrasound. The plan was to discontinue the daily progesterone and begin the progesterone injections and return in one month. My cervix was perfect and we were pregnant with another precious baby girl. Chris and I sat in the office and called our families to inform them of the great news! My Mom was so excited!!!

Chris's dream of our family portrait was coming more into focus. We were the parents of two little girls.

Two days after my appointment I started having lower back pain. I dismissed it as a urinary tract infection and started taking cranberry pills, which seemed to help. On Sunday morning, we decided to skip church. Chris had pulled a muscle in his leg and I was still having some back pain. We both decided to get some rest. By the afternoon we felt better and decided to go to the baby store to look for nursery furniture. It was the best of times!

We roamed every aisle looking at strollers, bassinets, cribs, comforters, and anything else that would be perfect for our daughter. It was such a good day. I found a lavender comforter embossed with the most delicate purple butterflies and immediately knew that's what I wanted for our daughter's nursery. Suddenly, I had some different movements. I felt frequent vibrations or tremors inside my stomach and pelvis. I was certain it wasn't fetal movement, but wondered what the feeling could be. Whatever the feeling was, it was something I had not felt before. I headed to the restroom, thinking if I relieve some pressure from my bladder it would likely alleviate the unending tremors.

I held my breath after I wiped. Slowly, I looked at the toilet paper hoping for the absence of blood. To my relief there was nothing! 'Exhale, Tanika,' I said to myself. Somehow, I needed another courtesy wipe just to make sure there was no blood. The second and third wipe brought me the peace I needed to resume our browsing experience in the store. "Is everything okay?" Chris asked.

"Yeah, I am just feeling some weird vibrations. Maybe the baby is sitting on a nerve or something," I exhaled.

We started looking at changing tables and dressers when the vibrations intensified. "I'll be back; I need to go to the restroom again. I'm feeling more vibrations."

Hurriedly, I walked to the restroom and wondered what our little tiny princess could be doing to cause such a riot. I sat in the bathroom and noticed how rapidly my heart was pounding. I said a prayer in my head, but couldn't synchronize my lips to articulate what I wanted to say. I sat on the toilet and braced myself for the worse. When I wiped the tissue appeared to be the same as before; totally normal. So I wiped again and the result was the same. Sitting quietly in the stall, I stared at the floor tile and wondered what could possibly be going on. Time escaped me and the sound of incoming bathroom visitors jolted me out of the panic-induced daze.

Chris was waiting outside of the restroom with a concerned look. "Are you okay?" he asked again.

"I really don't know what's going on, but I think we need to go home now."

We immediately left the store and headed for the car. I reclined my seat and sat quietly during the drive home. "Babe, what are you feeling?"

I made an honest attempt to articulate the strangeness that alarmed me. "The best way that I can describe it is a shaking feeling, almost like my stomach is trembling. I don't know if this is what a contraction feels like or not. It doesn't feel normal. I just want to go home and lie down. Perhaps that'll help."

As planned, I navigated myself directly to our bedroom and elevated my feet with as many pillows as I could find. I was hoping that my change in position would alleviate the pelvic distress I felt. The bedroom was perfectly quiet, except for the sound of the rapidly beating snare drum in my chest. I had to somehow redirect my mind to a tranquil place, before anxiety and panic further entangled me.

Music coupled with prayer had always proven to be the perfect medication for my anxiety. I closed my eyes, gripped my trembling belly and softly lifted the words, *"When peace like a river attendeth my way; when sorrows like sea billows roll. Whatever my lot, Thou has taught me to say, It is well; It is well with my soul."*

The tears flowed from my eyes and into my ears as I sensed that all was not well. "God, please," I petitioned, having only the strength to utter those two simple words before falling asleep.

Within in minutes of drifting off into the peace I longed for, my body sounded a terrifying alarm. For the first time, I felt abdominal and pelvic pain in addition to the trembling. Could this be a contraction? Slowly and with great caution, I eased into our living room to inform Chris of my suspicion. "Babe, I'm not for certain, but I think I am having contractions. I have more pain than before and the trembling is happening more frequently."

Chris immediately moved to action and suggested that we call the doctor just to be sure that everything was okay. Standing for those brief few moments caused me to feel the urgency to use the restroom. I scurried to the guest bathroom and made it just in the nick of time. The final wipe sent me in to sheer panic as I noticed thick, pale, yellow mucus on the paper. It was strong and had the texture of stretchy pasta. I examined every inch of the mucous and wiped again to see if there was any bleeding. Thankfully, there was no bleeding, but the mucus was concerning.

I called Dr. Laurel and the answering service advised me that he was not on call, but that another practice physician would be covering. I was put through to the pager of the covering OB. Forty minutes passed and my call was not returned, so I paged again. After not receiving a return call, we loaded the car and headed to the hospital.

Chapter 8
Dream Derailed

We arrived at the hospital and proceeded immediately to the Labor and Delivery floor where Dana, one of the charge nurses wheeled me to a room. I lifted my head and saw that we were headed into room 439, I screamed, "Please don't take me in that room!!!" I covered my face with my hands and wept openly. Flashbacks of emptiness, pain, and a lifeless baby quickly scrolled through my mind like an action packed movie.

Dana firmly rubbed my shoulder with empathy and compassion. There was no way she could have remembered either our previous admission to the hospital or our room assignment. I'm sure she had roomed several hundred expectant mothers who had been discharged with more favorable outcomes. However, my cry of despair changed her course of action. Without hesitation, she wheeled me into room 436 across the hall and apologized profusely.

Once Dana got me into the room the nurses moved speedily to assess my emergent situation. Chris and I explained the events of the day. I was examined by a doctor I had never met before. To our dismay, we learned that the only two medical professionals that knew our history firsthand, Dr. Laurel and Dr. Halton, were on vacation for the next seven days.

The on-call OB was very matter of fact, callous and unsympathetic in his introduction and findings. "Your bag of water is bulging through your cervix. There is nothing to do tonight, except watch and wait. We will place your bed in Trendelenburg position, so that your feet are fifteen to thirty degrees higher than your head.

"There is a very slim chance that this position will allow the bag of water to recede and we can perform a vaginal cerclage tomorrow. I'm going to start you on intravenous antibiotics immediately. My rounding partner will see you in the morning when he assumes my call. Do you have any questions?"

A wrecking ball had just landed on our chests! Of course, we had numerous questions. Our main questions were: What is cerclage and how is it placed? Secondly: What is the likelihood of the bag receding and continuing the pregnancy? We received the mile high educational moment on the cerclage and were told that the probability of a viable birth considering our present condition and increased chance of infection was less than five percent.

Seemingly, all of the odds were stacked against us. We had no further questions for him, yet we needed more information and a more positive vibe. Chris gripped my hand tighter as I stared at the ceiling while tears rolled down my face. "It's going to be okay, Babe." I closed my eyes and his words echoed in my mind and heart.

Dana heard everything that was said and sat on the bed beside me placing her warm hand over our gripped hands. "I know that wasn't the news you all wanted to hear. He gave you all a lot of information. Do you have any questions that I can try to answer?" Thankfully, Dana had the time to engage with us and didn't seem the least bit annoyed at our naive questions or our intermittent weeping. She was cut from the same cloth of compassion as Dr. Laurel and Halton. Her presence was powerful and her personal professionalism was the ray of light we needed in such a dark hour.

Chris and I settled in for the night, deciding to inform our families after we knew more news the next morning. A fetal and contraction monitor was placed around my belly, IV antibiotics were started and oral medications were given to stop the contractions. My bed was reclined to the prescribed position with my feet above my head. Chris prayed for the three of us and we tried to rest our minds and bodies.

All night I watched the hands on the clock slowly dance in a circular motion. Since I couldn't sleep, I surveyed the footsteps of each person walking by our room. A nurse came in to check on me at three a.m. "Have you been able to get any sleep?"

"No, I'm wide awake, I can't sleep," I replied. The on-call physician ordered something to help me sleep, which I had previously declined. The nurse suggested I take something to help me relax and to get some rest. I consented and was asleep soon after taking the medication.

Shift change came and I was not ready to open my eyes to face the day. I wanted to reach for the "do not disturb" sign and place it on the door, but I realized I was not at a five-star hotel. I was in the hospital and the folks there had a job to do. Suzanna Greene was my new day shift nurse. I immediately connected with her. She seemed so genuine and caring. She introduced herself and told us she would be taking care of us for the day. My vitals were checked, blood was drawn, and new IV fluids and antibiotics were hung. Suzanna informed me that the doctor was on the floor making rounds and he would be in to see me soon.

From the looks of Chris's position on the lounger and the snoring, I knew he slept well. "Babe, wake up, I need your help. The doctor will be in soon."

I was hopeful, having no contractions during the night. Since I wasn't in anymore pain, I was fairly convinced that all was well. The new rounding physician was old and had a very thick, white unibrow. "Good Morning, I'm Dr. Lewis. I'll be checking on you today."

Dr. Lewis gave an account of our history as he knew it from the report of the prior rounding physician and my medical record. "I need to do an internal exam to determine if your bag of water receded during the right," he said in a rushed, aggravated tone.

Chris and I held hands as the exam began. My eyes stretched wide and I sank my teeth into my bottom lip as his gargantuan hand navigated through such a delicate space. "Deep breaths, deep breaths, deeper breaths," I recited to myself silently during the exam.

As he examined me I watched for a favorable facial expression to appear on his stoic face, but there was none. "Alright, I'm done," he said removing the glove from his hand.

"Reclining in the Trendelenburg position did you no good. Your amniotic sac is hour glassed between your cervix and vagina," he said before giving us two options that we needed to decide between quickly.

The first option was to do nothing and wait for my body to go into labor naturally. I would need to continue antibiotics because the bag of water was already exposed and at risk for infection for both me and the baby. Our second option was the vaginal cerclage, which would need to be performed in several hours.

Chris and I knew we had to aggressively try to save our daughter. "We want the cerclage!!!"

Dr. Lewis explained that he would sedate me and manually, but ever so gently, attempt to maneuver the sac back into the cervix. After the process was complete, he could sew a purse string stitch around my cervix to prevent the bag of water from falling through the cervix. We discussed the associated risks, but still we were compelled to proceed with the surgery.

The time had come for us to put our faith on the line for a miracle. Our hope and faith in God was renewed and that's what had to carry us through the uncertainty we faced. Once again we made contact with our families and close friends to solicit their prayers.

Momma hurried to the hospital without delay and gave us a light scolding for not contacting her when we were admitted. I watched the clock tick hour by hour and prayed. My surgery was scheduled for two o'clock. Therefore, I counted down the hours until my womb was safe again and eagerly waited for the surgery to be over so that I could eat something; anything, actually.

A well dressed, soft spoken staff member asked if she could come in. She introduced herself as Cynthia Pope, one of the chaplains at the hospital. She wanted to know about us, how we were doing, and the events that led us to our current situation. Specifically, she wanted to know if she could pray with us before the surgery. I'm sure she didn't plan to spend nearly an hour with us, but I was grateful for her presence.

Once Chris and I connected with her we opened up and answered all her questions. During the conversation, Chris decided to step out of the room for a moment in search of coffee, which he desperately needed. Cynthia insisted on getting his coffee and bringing it back to our room. I never saw the job description for the hospital chaplain, but I was convinced that brewing a fresh pot of coffee and delivering it to the patient's room was not one of the core responsibilities. Clearly, Chaplain Cynthia was cut from the same cloth of compassion as Dr. Laurel, Dr. Halton, Suzanna, and Dana.

While we were chatting, the anesthesia team came to place my epidural and prepare me for surgery. Cynthia's visit was the perfect distraction and just what we needed to calm the silent anxiety that we masked with a charismatic smile and conversation. "Can I pray with them really quickly before you take her?" Cynthia asked the anesthesia staff. Her angelic voice powerfully and passionately prayed for mercy, grace and blessings for us, our families, and for the medical team who would care for us.

Momma kissed my forehead and told me that I would be okay. Chris and I exchanged a quick hug and kiss and I was being wheeled out of the door. "I love you and I'll be here when you get back." Seeing the look of uncertainty frame his face moved me to tears. Cynthia told me that she'd stay with Chris and Momma for a while longer.

I arrived to a cold, white operating room and was placed on a very thin surgical table. Looking at the small table, I was not convinced that it would hold my full framed figure. I remember oxygen being applied to my face, looking up at the white light and being told to relax. I confirmed that I could not feel the cold metal instrument on my legs. The time had come for the surgery to begin.

"One, two, three," I heard in my subconscious mind as I drifted into deep sleep as the procedure began. They had placed me onto the hospital bed and warm blankets were applied to my chest. When I opened my eyes they were wheeling me back to my room. Thankfully, I did not feel much pain, but I was most certainly relaxed.

71

My room was empty and I had no idea where Chris was. I floated back off to enjoy the sleep I should have earlier, but was interrupted by shift change. Cynthia came into the room and informed me that Chris went to grab some lunch and would be back soon. "Can I have his cell phone number to let him know that you've returned from surgery?" she asked.

"Yes, it's 972-4...," was all I could say before returning to my peaceful slumber.

When I woke up Chris' sweaty hand was rubbing my forehead. "Babe, wake up the doctor is here."

I squinted and scratched my head in an effort to wake up. My eyes were wide as I surveyed the multitude of people around the bedside. Cynthia, Chris, Momma, Dr. Lewis, and two other people I did not recognize were gazing at me. Dr. Lewis cleared his throat. "Tanika, I attempted the cerclage. As I told you earlier, it is a delicate procedure that has some risks involved, which you were willing to take in order to save the pregnancy. Unfortunately, the bag of water ruptured immediately as I touched it. There was nothing more we could do at that time but discontinue the procedure."

I removed Chris's hand from my head and gripped it with every fiber of strength that remained in me. I dropped my head as tears gathered under my chin like waves crashing against the shore.

"What can we do now?" I asked.

"Your body will start to labor naturally now that your water has broken. We will not do anything to stop the laboring process and anticipate that you will deliver sometime tonight."

I was physically numbed from the anesthesia and emotionally numbed from the unexpected, devastating news. There were absolutely no words that I could formulate to ask a question or respond to Dr. Lewis in any way. Each thought I had in my head floated with the stream of tears that fell. Chris sat on the bed and held me close to his chest while I openly sobbed.

BUILDING A FAMILY BREAKS MY HEART

I wept for our daughter who was struggling to survive in an environment where she should have thrived. I wept for Chris and the plans that he had to spoil our daughter, just as he had spoiled me. I wept for derailed dreams that had matured into life-sized nightmares. I wept for what should have been, but could never be. I wept for the perfect family photo Chris envisioned that would never be mounted on our wall. Grief apprehended me and there was no escape.

Cynthia was in the room as a quiet, yet powerful presence, as we sorrowed. She asked if she could explain a few of the services that were offered through the "Tiny Touches" program for children that are born with a small chance of survival or who had died in utero. She also explained the services of the Pastoral Care Department, as she represented both departments. We were most interested in having our child blessed and giving her a name, but we did not want an official ceremony. While we did not have to make any decisions right away, we were thankful that we knew all of the information beforehand.

We wanted to spend each precious moment with our daughter when she arrived rather than being inundated with information. Since such a short amount of time had passed since the gender ultrasound, we had not given much thought to a name, but now felt we had to forge through our emotions and decide on one. I sat in the bed and gripped my stomach and wondered about our daughter's personality, who she would resemble the most and what she would be as an adult. I gazed at the ceiling and floor tiles and gave great thought to a name, but I simply could not think of anything meaningful.

Seemingly, out of nowhere, Chris stated, "I like the name Briauna."

"Why do you like that name?" I asked, surprised by his matter-of-fact tone.

"I'm not sure, but I like it."

Chris's response was good enough for me. I immediately remembered that Ebriauna was one of the nine names of my children that I had written down in my journal when I was in the ninth grade. Despite the small variations of the name, I was completely agreeable to Chris's suggestion. Our daughter had a name! "What goes well with Briauna for a middle name?" I asked.

Without hesitation Chris replied, "Angel." I did not need an explanation for his rationale and agreed to Briauna Angel Dillard.

One major task was completed on our list. Naming Briauna did not seem difficult, but naming her sister who had not been in my arms in nearly eight months would be a challenge. It simply would not be fair, in my opinion, to have a nameless oldest child and a name for the second child. So, Chris and I dialogued about the name for a few brief moments. He liked the name "Mary Elizabeth," for his daughter before we ever conceived a child. He thought the name was strong and noble. I adamantly protested and exercised the power of veto to declare that I would never name my child such a classic, outdated name. We had to agree on a more modern name and leave "Mary Elizabeth" to the mothers of Jesus and John the Baptist.

Chris liked the name Destiny, which was also listed as one of my children's names in my journal. I could not recall having any negative encounters with anyone named Destiny, but I was no longer enthusiastic about the name in the least way. I loved the name "Almaray" because it was the fusion of both of my dear Grandmas' names: Alma and Rachel. I could not think of another name to give our daughter other than Almaray. She should be named after the two ladies who loved me so much and helped to shape my life.

Each time I envisioned our little girl in heaven, she was in the arms of one of my Grandmas. Destiny Alamray was approved as the name for our firstborn daughter. After being called "our baby" or "our daughter" for eight months, Destiny finally had a name and I was proud of the name we had given her.

I began to labor naturally, just as Dr. Lewis suspected. It was amazing how my body automatically knew to expand and stretch, but did not know how to protect and shield the little life inside of me. The brilliance of my body amazed me and the incompetence of my body angered me.

Word had spread to our friends and family about the unsuccessful surgery and impending delivery. Text messages, phone calls and emails of support poured in from across the east coast. Our beloved Pastor Williams stopped by to visit us and encourage our frail hearts. He did not come into our room with the goal of explaining God or why this happened to us. He told us he didn't know why this happened to us again and he would never try to spiritualize our pain. However, he assured us that in time, God would use our pain for His glory and we may have a better understanding of His plan.

I trusted Pastor's words, just as I had trusted the words he spoke over my life since I became a member of his church eleven years prior. Pastor stood by my bedside and prayed with such fervor and expectancy that God would hear all of the petitions for us and grant us a divine miracle. By the end of the prayer, I felt a warm fluid between my legs. Pastor left and the door sealed closed. I immediately pushed my call light and asked for my nurse to come. I told Momma and Chris that something was wrong.

Allison quickly entered the room. "I think it's time," I said as I pulled back the white blanket to show her the bright red blood on my gown and the sheets. She grabbed her stethoscope and checked for a heartbeat but did not find one.

Allison shook her head and said, "I'm sorry Hun, I'll go call the doctor."

A team of medical professionals rushed into the room bringing medical supplies, IV fluids, a bassinet and many other items. "I feel a lot of pressure, almost like I have to use the restroom." I was so uncomfortable, but was reassured that everything that I felt was normal.

Dr. Lewis soon arrived and performed an internal check. After several hours of labor I was dilated enough to deliver our silent daughter. I did not push – my body was performing a self evacuation without any assistance from me. "Ten thirty-seven p.m." one of the nurses said quietly.

Our daughter had made a quiet entrance into the world. She was immediately whisked away to an incubator to be checked for any signs of life. There were no cries and no shouts of victory. The room was virtually silent with the exception of my chattering teeth and panting. My body began to violently shake as Dr. Lewis attempted to deliver the placenta.

The pressure and discomfort I felt earlier had transformed into pain. Dr. Lewis called for an increase in IV medication and forceps. My eyes stretched wide as I felt the intensity of the force being used to birth the placenta. Chris steadied his hand upon my chest in an attempt to control the involuntary shaking. "Doctor, she is shaking really bad. Is this normal?" he asked.

"Yes, it's the normal reaction to her body responding to trauma," Dr. Lewis responded.

The procedure finally came to a welcomed end. Momma draped me in several warm blankets she had gathered from the nurses' desk. I closed my eyes and could only hear Chris gently reassuring me, "It's okay, just breathe. Calm down, you're okay." My husband's words helped my rapidly beating heart to return to normal.

"Would you like to see your baby now?" Allison asked.

"Yes, please," I whispered.

She wheeled our daughter close to my bed and gave us a basket and two crochet blankets that we could use to drape her if we wanted pictures. I carefully lifted our tiny, fragile little girl from the blood stained blanket. "Hey, Precious Girl, we didn't expect to see you so soon." I examined her tiny fingers and toes. I looked intently at her entire body, which fit my hand like a glove. She was perfect in every way, just born too soon. She had Chris's nose and my long legs. I could only dream and imagine what she might have become.

Thankfully, we packed our camera in the overnight bag. We took a few pictures of her. I knew I wouldn't remember the details of her little body or appearance. I had to have some way to remember her aside from relying on mental images. As much as I took in every detail of our firstborn daughter Destiny, I could only vaguely and painfully remember anything about her features. I did not want to rely on my memory again.

Chris captured a picture of her tiny hand in mine, pictures of her fingers and toes, pictures of her in my hands and her seven-ounce body. Momma held Briauna in her hands and softly spoke with excitement to her as if she were alive. "Nana loves her little Angel Girl, yes she does," she proclaimed as she rocked back and forth. She made certain to have a lengthy conversation with Briauna to let her know of all of her cousins on earth and how much everyone loved her.

I often envisioned Momma with my children as I watched her with my nephew and nieces. I knew that she would officially be the Spoiler-in-Chief of our children. Never once had I imagined that she wouldn't have the opportunity to buy frilly dresses, tights, earrings, bows, and miniature fur coats to match hers. Seeing Momma at my bedside with our daughter, hearing her voice tremble as she held back tears hurt just as much as the delivery I had just experienced. In that moment, life seemed so unfair and the sting of death was evident.

As empty as I felt during those dark moments, crying was never an option. I only had a limited time with our daughter and I was not going to waste a second of that time crying. We had moments to enjoy and memories to make. We sang to our beloved child and filled a few hours with a lifetime of love. We told her about her sister and her great-grandmothers that would be waiting for her in heaven. I wanted her to know that she would never be alone. I asked our tiny messenger to kiss her big sister for us and thank my grandmas for taking care of them.

The entrance of a new day came and we were unaware of its arrival. Our bodies were beyond the point of physical, mental, and emotional exhaustion. The nurse brought pillows and blankets into our room and converted Chris's recliner into a sleeper. She offered me some medicine to help me sleep as she could see that I was physically tired, but emotionally wired.

Momma gathered her belongs and prepared to leave for home. She held the basket which held her little "Angel Girl" and shook her head in silence and stretched her eyes wide as if to prevent the tears from falling. There were no appropriate words to say goodbye. Momma was silent, but her eyes spoke on her behalf. She embraced Chris and me so tightly that she trembled. She assured us that we would get through the pain, told us she loved us and would see us the next morning. Chris walked her to the car and the tears I had successfully withheld became fully engaged.

Chris returned to the room to find a display of emotional chaos. There were no words spoken. He quietly eased next to me on the bed and held me with all of his might. Our nurse returned with my medicine and offered to take Briauna for the night so we could rest. I accepted the offer for the medicine, but decided that our daughter should remain with us for as long as possible. We were simply not ready to say goodbye.

My eyes grew heavy from the combination of pain medication and the sleeping aide. As much as I tried to fight the exhaustion, I was powerless. I switched my bed light off, reclined my bed and eased the tiny basket containing my sleeping baby girl, Briauna close to me. I slept peacefully through the night and only woke up when the nursing staff made rounds to check on us.

Morning light came sooner than I wanted it to appear. I already knew I would be discharged from the hospital and sent home to face reality. However, we had many decisions to make prior to our departure. Cynthia dropped in for a visit and we were glad to see her. She was genuinely concerned and interested to know how Chris and I were doing emotionally and physically. Cynthia was ever so careful with her words and wanted to be respectful of our feelings. She brought in two angel bears for each of our daughters, not wanting us to leave the hospital with empty arms. I knew those bears would never replace Destiny and Briauna;

however, the compassion Cynthia showed us touched the darkest part of our hurting hearts.

Cynthia asked if we had made a decision for a funeral or graveside service. Since we opted to let Destiny's remains be sent to the genetics labs for testing and disposal, we could not, in good conscience hold a service for Briauna. We wanted to be fair to both of the girls although they would never know the decisions we made. Cynthia completely understood and did not even offer a rebuttal. There was a program offered at the hospital to privately and sacredly bury all babies who were born due to fetal demise who fit a certain criteria. Briauna met the criteria for this compassionate option and we decided to proceed with that offer.

We completed all of the remaining paperwork and prepped for discharge. My heart raced at the mere thought of leaving the hospital again without carrying a baby in my arms. The emptiness in Chris's eyes made my eyes fill with tears. Life seemed so very unfair in that moment as our lifeless daughter lay on a blanket-covered basket by the sink.

All of our belongings were packed in our suitcase and we were given an additional purple bag filled with Briauna's memory box, keepsakes from Cynthia, the crocheted blankets that kept Briauna's body warm and a sympathy card from the staff. We were grateful for everything that had been given to us to preserve Briauna's memory, but I wanted to scream in protest. I did not want memories; I wanted my daughter for heaven's sake!!!

Suzanna brought in a wheelchair and asked if I was ready to go as I stood next to Briauna's little body at the sink. I was not prepared to go, but there was no reason for me to stay. "I can walk out rather than riding in the wheelchair," I said in a quiet voice.

I did not want people to know that I was leaving the Labor and Delivery floor with a *"purple bag."* Walking out would not disclose our misfortune to anyone. "I'm sorry, but it is our policy to wheel you down and it's for your safety," Suzanna explained.

I understood and slowly eased into the wheelchair and fixed my eyes on the basket. Tears began to roll down my face again as Suzanna unlocked the wheelchair. "You let me know when you are ready, okay. Just take your time," she said in a soothing voice, rubbing my back. She then placed a box of Kleenex on my lap.

"Are you okay, Chris?" she asked as she patted him on the back.

"Oh, yeah, I'm fine. Thank you."

After a brief moment of silence, I informed Suzanna that we could leave. She slowly began to step backwards with the wheelchair. I could do nothing but shake my head and close my eyes. The room was dark and empty, much like me. We proceeded up the hallway towards the elevators and I opened my eyes in time enough to see room 439. The door was opened and I remembered so well my departure and the feelings that accompanied it.

As we approached the elevators, I heard conversations and laughter. Those families had likely just experienced a birth or were awaiting the arrival of an impending birth. I was ashamed that I had nothing, so I dropped my head as far as I could and covered my eyes with my hand. Thankfully, the elevator arrived quickly and I was relieved to hear the doors open.

Chris drove the car to the entrance of the building while Suzanna and I waited. She gave me a few reminders from my discharge instructions and encouraged me to call back to the floor if I needed anything. Chris arrived with the car and Suzanna began to assist me out of the wheelchair. I took two steps and stopped to give her one final hug. "Thank you for everything. We'll be back to see you soon." Suzanna hugged Chris and encouraged him to call the floor if he needed anything also and I smiled through the tears for the first time.

CHAPTER 9
Be Strong

My entire body was drained and my cervix was obviously weak to the point of repetitive failure. My body was weak from pain. My eyes were weak from crying. My strength was weak. Everything was weak with the exception of my faith. Yet, I still had hopes of bringing a baby home alive and building the family empire I had dreamed of at Grandma's house. I still had hopes of being a mother and the matriarch of the family. I still had hopes of nursing a baby upon my breast. Our daughters died, but the dream within me was still alive.

My faith was shaken, because I didn't expect the outcome to be as it was. I believed that God heard our prayers and the prayers of our family and friends. I trusted God just as much as I did when I was a little girl sitting on the heater at Grandma's house. *'Most assuredly, God would not let another bad tragedy happen to us,'* I thought. When all of the hope within my heart was shattered, I had no choice but to pick up the broken pieces and give them back to God. I was broken and in need of the process of mending.

Now I was angry that I still believed, even after two needless losses, that God would indeed give us children. I spoke aloud to myself asking, "Why do you still believe?" I had heard heart wrenching stories of others who had experienced losses that had happy endings. So, I trusted that it could happen for us also. I trusted that God loved us and that He would give us the desires of our heart. I trusted that the worst was over and we were on our way to brighter days.

Again, I often wondered how Chris held his composure so well. I never saw him shed a tear with the losses of our daughters. Chris was physically strong, but his emotional strength often puzzled me. He always made me his number one priority. He made sure I ate and took my medicines, held me during the night as I cried, and listened to the words that flowed from my broken heart. He never told me how to feel or minimized my pain. Instead, he gave me permission to be completely weak – he was my safe place.

In my heart, I wanted Chris to feel exactly what I did. I wanted to see him show emotion so that I wouldn't feel like the only one who was grieving in our home. He was my safe haven and I wanted to be the same to him while he grieved. I would ask open-ended questions to spark some dialogue as to how he was genuinely feeling. Despite my efforts, his responses were often one word answers. He didn't want to talk about his feelings with me and it made me very angry. I couldn't understand how we could both lose pieces of ourselves and not be able to communicate together about our feelings.

Eventually, he explained that he grieved in his own way whenever he was alone. "Baby, I have to be strong for you."

"Why do you have to be strong for me? Neither one of us has to be strong!!!" I protested.

Almost immediately, I understood his plight. The medical staff at the hospital saw him as a grieving father, everyone else saw him only as the supporter and husband to a grieving wife. All I heard was, "Chris, be strong – take care of Tanika," more times than I care to recall. The few visitors would firmly pat him on the back and charge him to be strong.

Clearly from the public's point of view, men are not supposed to grieve. While I was encouraged to take all the time I needed, Chris was commissioned to quickly thrust himself back into life as usual. My blood flowed through my veins like hot lava each time I heard such an insensitive comment from the lips of those who couldn't comprehend the weight of our losses. I wanted to scream, "Be strong for what and for whom?!"

My logic for wanting Chris to feel exactly what I felt was unfavorably skewed. He didn't have the capacity to feel or understand why I cried when my breasts were engorged and leaked milk. There was no understanding as to why I felt like my body was playing a cruel trick on me. I was still feeling fetal movement inside of my stomach, although

Briauna's body was in a mass grave with other babies. My husband didn't understand why I cried at the sight of my unclothed body as I saw a round stomach that still looked like it contained a baby. Every month when my cycle returned, I cried. I was angry with my body for betraying me. I cried when my hair began to shed and my nails broke after discontinuing the prenatal vitamins. I cried at the sight of pregnant strangers and wondered why they were lucky enough to keep their children, but we could not.

In time, I realized that we each needed to grieve, but had to do it in our own unique way. Though we shared the same experiences, we processed them differently. Chris felt the need to maintain the stability of our household emotionally, spiritually, and financially. He couldn't pass his role as provider and protector to someone else, nor could he place his role on indefinite pause while he grieved. Quite frankly, my husband felt like he didn't have time to grieve.

In the meantime, I resorted to being pseudo-balanced in his presence so he wouldn't feel compelled to be my emotional support. Despite my best efforts, I could not break into his emotions. He refused to allow me to see him broken because it is a law in the, *"How a Real Man Should Behave,"* imaginary book. Whenever he was having a moment he'd retreat into our office with his Bible for hours. Perhaps it was his way of gaining strength. It was confirmed by his heartfelt, "Hallelujah, thank You Lord!" echoing through the door. His spiritual strength and positive perspective were noteworthy, but they caused me to wonder if he was angry with God as much as I was.

We still loved and trusted God, but I felt like He dangled promises before us and suddenly snatched them away without cause. I was angry that God would allow us to hurt so deeply. I was angry that so many prayers were seemingly discarded. As angry and disappointed as I was with God, I still needed Him. We certainly needed Him if we were ever going to recover from the darkness that hung over us. Many days during my six-week maternity leave, I'd stand in the shower or at the kitchen sink with tears streaming down my face, singing hymns. Seemingly, the words of, *"I Need Thee,"* captured the deepest longing in my soul.

Despite the charge Chris was given to be strong, I lacked the ability to be strong for him. We were completely weak, but perhaps weakness was exactly what we needed. Day by day we felt the strength of God restoring us to life as He had designed. We still had questions and I still cried as we were being lifted out of the darkness. As we rose from the ashes of pain I realized that 2 Corinthians 2:9 (KJV) had proven to be true. *"And he said unto me, My grace is sufficient for thee: for my strength is made perfect in weakness."*

Contrary to the repeated exhortations, I wished someone had encouraged Chris to be weak and given him permission to grieve. I wished someone told him that he had the right to cry without discrediting his manhood. I wished someone had told him that holding it together prolongs the healing process. I wished he never knew the expectations of others. Being strong is unnecessary when we have a God who is never depleted of strength.

Chapter 10
Removing The Mask

While in the presence of others I put forth great effort to be a non-grieving Tanika. I returned to my normal activities of work and church, but was far from normal. As days passed I questioned the progress of my grief recovery and emotional healing. I wanted to avoid baby showers, pregnant women, happy people, overly sympathetic people and co-workers who were glowing in pregnancy. I would respond to phone calls with an email and found a good excuse to send our regrets to every invitation we were given. I wasn't happy, but had hope and dreamed of a better, brighter day.

Eventually, I sought counseling for self-diagnosed depression, panic attacks, and social isolation. Counseling sessions were so frustrating. The counselor rephrased my statements of grief and anger, and then gave me assignments for the next session. I completed the assignments, which gave me a new perspective of my grief and helped me progress forward. The frustrating aspect of the counseling occurred when I returned for my next session. When I got there I'd have to ask the counselor if she wanted my homework. She'd read over my work, provided little to no feedback, and concluded our sessions by giving me another assignment. After several sessions, I decided not to continue.

My greatest outlet was talking my feelings out with Chris and other friends who had experienced pregnancy loss. I felt normal when I spoke with other mothers who knew the same grief. They understood exactly what I said and how I felt. I joined an online grief and loss message board/support group after losing Destiny. I'd read stories from those mothers and often found myself nodding in agreement – I understood them. I cried with them and was able to genuinely celebrate the announcements of their new arrivals and pregnancy without harboring any feelings of jealousy.

The message board was filled with many different pregnancy and loss experiences. Support for each other was overwhelming and the educational exchange and dialogue was greater than any classroom could ever be. I read numerous success stories from other mothers like myself who had lost multiple children due to an incompetent cervix. They would post glowing pregnancy pictures and their miracle babies. The common thread and most-endorsed treatment within the group was the cerclage.

A Transvaginal Cerclage (TVC) or a Transabdominal Cerclage (TAC) was necessary to ensure the reinforcement of the cervix. The TVC, which Dr. Lewis attempted during my pregnancy, was most often followed by prolonged bed rest in order to carry the baby to term. All of the stories were the same: multiple losses, pregnancy, TVC, bed rest, birth of a baby and possibly a stay in the NICU. From the information I gathered online, the TAC seemed to be the best route. It was most commonly placed after multiple losses, but prior to a subsequent pregnancy. The overall success rate was nearly 100% and many expectant mothers enjoyed full-term pregnancies without bed rest.

Armed with a plan for our next pregnancy, I was determined to be my own advocate and chart my course for success in building our family. I scheduled an appointment with Dr. Halton and prepared nearly twenty questions to ask during my consultation, making sure he carefully and honestly answered each one of them. "When can I get the transabdominal cerclage placed?" I asked with great excitement.

"Oh, you won't need that. The transvaginal cerclage will work. Besides, I don't want you to have to go through the surgery, recovery, and expense of the abdominal procedure. I won't pull out the "big guns," unless we see that you really need it." His response was anything but music to my ears.

With a raised brow I asked, "So, are you saying that I have to lose another baby before I can have a transabdominal cerclage?"

Dr. Halton assured me that he would personally perform my TVC and we would be okay. I presented a good argument, or so I thought, but my desire was no match to Dr. Halton's years of education and experience. After our conversations we established a plan to move forward. The event planner inside of me had to know the big picture down to the smallest of details.

During my next pregnancy my cervix would be monitored closely. The cerclage would be placed during the twelfth week of pregnancy, followed by bi-weekly cervical measurements until delivery. I would start progesterone injections at sixteen weeks. If at any time my cervix measured below two point five centimeters, I'd be placed on bed rest until delivery. An amniocentesis would be performed at thirty-seven weeks. Once the baby's lungs were developed, the cerclage would be removed and we would simply wait for my body to go into natural labor.

Dr. Halton was hopeful and excited at the very thought of closing the Labor and Delivery Unit in order to throw a huge welcome party for our miracle baby whenever he or she arrived. I trusted his medical expertise and the commitment to do everything in his power to ensure that we had the opportunity to be parents that take a living baby home. I saw hope in his eyes and a glimpse of hope funneled through my heart.

Once Dr. Halton soothed my fears, I asked Cynthia if there was a support group at the hospital. I knew I didn't want to try the counseling route again, but wanted some kind of outlet that would enable me to move forward in a healthy manner. There had been a group in the past, but it had since dissipated for various reasons. There was also a small group from another local hospital who met regularly, but Cynthia wasn't certain of the details.

Since Cynthia was connected to another local hospital, she proposed that the two form a joint support group. She envisioned joining forces to maximize effectiveness and meet the needs of the growing number of grieving families in our area. The idea quickly moved from Cynthia's head to her heart. She began the massive undertaking of establishing a local chapter of a national support group in South Carolina. This support group would be the first chapter in the state.

In order to help Cynthia's vision materialize, I was willing to put my administrative and clerical skills to work. However, she envisioned a parent-led support group and targeted me to be the representative. When she made the suggestion, I had absolutely no experience with leading support groups. However, I did have experience in leading people, supporting someone else's vision and supporting others who had experienced the loss of a baby.

In no time, I was completing the group's application with Cynthia, sitting in on advisory meetings and conference calls. I was excited to be an integral part of the group's framework. Everything was happening very fast, but it all seemed so very right. Cynthia's invitation was exactly what I needed to refocus my life and emotional stability. My personal and professional life returned to baseline, where happiness and optimism flourished.

Chapter 11
Back To the Basics

While we desperately wanted to establish our family, we took time to focus on each other and the love we shared. Grief can take a toll on relationships and create communication barriers. Finally, Chris and I were able to laugh again. We dated again. We dreamed again and most importantly we loved each other deeper than we ever had before. We returned to the basics of love and life. I had a greater appreciation for quiet evenings at home with no prearranged activities. We intentionally discovered each other's love language and seized every opportunity to make each other smile. Simple gestures of love spoke volumes. Saying, "I love you," just because, giving an unexpected hug or a card to say, "I appreciate you," awakened a great passion within us. We were committed to making a happy life by loving deeply and completely.

After eight months of reconnecting we were happily pregnant with baby number three. April twenty-first marked the day of a new beginning. I calculated the date of conception and our due date. The baby was immediately named Love Bug as he or she was conceived on the anniversary of our dating and engagement. The stars were aligned and Love Bug was due December 22nd, just days after Briauna's due date of December 28th of the previous year.

This time would be different and we both knew it. We spoke of our faith to everyone we shared our exciting news with. I immediately called Dr. Laurel's office and anxiously awaited an appointment to confirm the pregnancy and have an ultrasound to see the tiniest little miracle inside of me. My laboratory and blood results were perfect. I was prescribed progesterone to ensure that my level would stay in an acceptable range and prevent an early miscarriage.

Once again everybody was excited, and they all encouraged us. We knew our family, friends and medical team were praying for us. Everyone was equally vested in our pregnancy. Chris and I were determined to enjoy every moment of pregnancy. We celebrated every milestone in our pregnancy and thanked God each night for the miracle of life.

We were anxious to have our first ultrasound. Janice, the scheduler at Dr. Halton's office, knew our history and made sure to schedule the appointment without delay. The ultrasound showed a minute miracle in the making. Our hearts leapt with joy!!! Krista, one of the sonographers at the office checked my cervical length and happily reported that it was normal. Everything was as it should be and we already had a plan in place for the course of the pregnancy. We were about six weeks away from the planned cerclage. The plan was coming together nicely.

My cousin, Maxine had a medical grade Doppler and offered to send it to us. She assured us that having a Doppler at our disposal would help to alleviate any worries we had. The bonus was that we could hear the beautiful melody of our child's heartbeat at anytime. I graciously accepted her offer without any hesitation. The Doppler arrived by priority mail just a few days after our conversation.

One afternoon Chris came to take me to lunch. When he arrived he had our mail for that day in the truck with him. And when I saw the package from Maxine, I ripped it open and reclined my seat. "Are you going to use that right now?" he asked.

"Yes, I want to hear this baby's heartbeat now," I said, lifting my shirt. I tucked it under my bra and lowered my pants to my pelvic bone. I applied the cold gel to my stomach, then pressed the wand just below my belly button. At first there was a great deal of static and I didn't hear a heartbeat. So, I moved the wand from right side to left and back again. Finally, we heard a faint heartbeat despite all of the crackles in the background. I couldn't decipher if it was my heartbeat or our baby's and didn't care. I was simply happy to hear something other than static.

Just before going to bed, I used it again. I thought lying completely flat would better help me locate the baby. My assumption was correct! After a few minutes of searching we both heard a very rapid heartbeat. That time I knew we were hearing the baby's heart and not mine. Tears filled my eyes as we listened to the soothing sound. We decided to make it our new tradition. At the end of every night we would listen to our Love Bug. I took a video of Chris singing "You are so Beautiful," on my mobile phone and some nights I would place it on my stomach and play the video until I fell asleep. There were other nights when Chris would place his hands on my stomach hoping to feel the baby and sing the ABC's. He would then pray God's protection over the both of us. We felt that it was important for our Love Bug to hear our voices consistently throughout the day.

During my tenth week of pregnancy I felt what seemed to be a flickering butterfly in my stomach. Most of the literature that I found suggested that fetal movement wouldn't be felt until twenty weeks. I just assumed I was hypersensitive to my changing body and noticed every detail. Feeling our baby move ignited such a level of happiness and excitement within me. I wanted Chris to feel the magic happening in my womb. However, my words were inadequate to describe what I was feeling. Despite using every adjective and descriptive word I knew, Chris was not moved to excitement by words alone. I couldn't wait for the day when he could feel exactly what I was speaking about.

Dr. Laurel and Dr. Halton monitored me closely. Every week I had an ultrasound and cervical measurement check. The plan for the cerclage placement at twelve weeks was reviewed in detail and had not changed. It seemed like we reached the twelfth week of pregnancy overnight. Everything moved at the speed of light!

The long awaited day for the cerclage placement finally arrived. Chris and I were both excited and relieved to have the safety net put in place to ensure a healthy baby came home with us. We were 100% confident in Dr. Halton's ability. He had successfully placed hundreds of vaginal cerclages in his career. We had a friend and former church member who had two precious children, partially because Dr.

Halton placed her cerclages successfully. Our case was to be just as routine as all the other surgical procedures. We were hopeful and excited to start this new chapter of pregnancy and in our lives.

Many of the nursing staff who had cared for Chris and I before stopped by our room to say a quick hello before the surgery. I almost felt like we were at a family reunion. The staff and I talked about what was going on in their lives and they congratulated us on being so fertile. Cynthia came to pray with us and to see how we were feeling. Our favorite nurse, Suzanna, was also there and stopped by for hugs and well wishes. We had become a family. Not only were we confident in our medical doctor, but also in the medical staff!

I was wheeled into the cold operating room and Julie, one of my former nurses, talked me through the administration of the spinal and helped to calm my nerves. Dr. Halton was calm and vibrant. His bright blue eyes were the same color as the sterile uniform he wore. He assured me that the placement wouldn't take long and both the baby and I would be fine, and I believed him!

Dr. Halton began the procedure as a familiar hit from the eighties played in the background. He whistled to the music and so did some of the surgical techs. We were all very relaxed and Dr. Halton let me know when he began delicately sowing the purse string around my cervix. "Make sure the stitch is tight," I said.

"This thing is not going anywhere – I made sure of it!"

My life had changed for the better in less than thirty minutes. I was wheeled back to my room to recover and Dr. Halton happily reported that the surgery went as planned. We knew the cerclage would provide for a more favorable outcome because of the condition of my cervix. He informed us of the precautions, which mainly included no lifting anything greater than five pounds and absolutely no sex for the duration of the pregnancy. Sex was prohibited, because it could negatively alter the functionality of the cerclage. The look of disappointment and ultimate dissatisfaction were clearly visible on Chris's face. I could see him subconsciously counting July, August, September, October, November, December and six weeks after recovery. It was sure to be an extremely long pregnancy for the both of us.

Within a few hours after my surgery we were being prepped for discharge. We said our goodbyes to the staff and I promised Julie and Suzanna that I would not see them again until it was time to deliver in December. For the first time in two and a half years, we were leaving the hospital with hope, excitement, optimism and a very active baby in utero. The black cloud that loomed over us had transformed into bright skies. Everything about the pregnancy seemed better and I wasn't paranoid or worried.

Although the gender ultrasound was still a few weeks away, I had an indescribable feeling that I was carrying another daughter. In fact, I was so confident that we would bring a baby girl home in December that I went to the shopping mall and purchased an adorable pink outfit with ruffles and a pair of pink and brown leopard print pants. I was drawn to girly things and there was also a baby girl in all of my dreams. I looked forward to the future and envisioned our daughter looking like Chris and having my dimples.

We were ready to pick out a name without delay. Surprisingly, we never even broached the subject of a name for a boy. Perhaps, it was the unspoken knowledge that our first son would be named after Chris or the very strong female intuition that I had. I liked the name Addison, but Chris on the other hand wasn't fond of my choice and proposed the name Madison. There was little dialogue about the name and I eventually conceded. I was adamant that Noelle should be her middle name since my due date was so close to Christmas. Madison Noelle Dillard had the perfect amount of magic for us. We were completely excited about the name and could not wait to confirm that our assumptions were right.

My recovery was quick and uneventful. I returned to work five days after my surgery, beaming with joy. My hope and faith were renewed. The heavy burden of worry had been placed far from me and my pregnancy progressed flawlessly. I looked fabulous, I felt amazing, and I was the happiest pregnant woman I knew. For the first time, I felt safe allowing Chris to take pictures of my growing belly and glowing face. I posed and imagined how much bigger I'd become in the coming twenty-five weeks.

The time had come for the official launch of the grief and loss support group. Ginger was my partner in leading the support group. She was the representative for the other hospital and helped me accept the task of leading the group. We stood before the advisory council comprised of professionals from both hospitals and were commissioned to lead the group with dignity and compassion. I felt extremely honored to be asked to lead other people who had been traveling down the same grief road as we had.

A few weeks following the commissioning service, we welcomed families into our first support group meeting. I was totally comfortable speaking with Chris, Cynthia, Momma and a few of my closest friends about our losses. But now I had a great deal of apprehension in sharing my gloomy story with absolute strangers. What if I cried too much in the meeting? What if I were the one who needed extra Kleenex, hugs and hand-holding in order to make it through the one and a half hour meeting? What if the sight of my second trimester belly bump caused other grieving moms to cry?

The more I thought about the countless "what ifs," the more I tried to talk myself out of attending the support group meeting. I allowed my mind to go back to the most painful places of our losses. Then I wondered if my story was too graphic or too much to share. How much information should I disclose and how much should I reserve for my own repertoire of grief? Finally, it was time for me to put my fears aside and head north to the church where we were to meet. I cried from the moment I left my house until a few minutes before arriving at the church.

Seeing Cynthia, Kay, and the other advisory members helped calm my nerves before the other grieving families arrived. I had to admit that I was nervous because I didn't know what to expect. However, I was equally excited at the opportunity to help others. Ginger and I created family relationships with those who came for the meeting. It was obvious that they too had shed tears while en route to the meeting. There were tearstained faces, red eyes, and trembling voices in every corner of the room. Clearly I was not alone in my emotions.

Kay opened the meeting with an eloquent welcome and a prayer. Her soothing voice seemed to draw us all into a sacred place. Ginger and I were introduced as the parent facilitators and we each shared a little about our journey and the children that led us to the support group. As I listened to each story, I felt empathy towards their grief and understood exactly how they felt. If given the opportunity, I could have finished their sentences for them. I also felt a relieving sense of validation. The mothers at the meeting were passionately verbalizing their experiences and how they managed to face each day. I found myself smiling and nodding in agreement as I realized that I wasn't overreacting in my own grief. Surely, I wasn't alone and ironically I felt connected to a room full of strangers. By the end of the night we were all friends bonded by grief and love.

Leaving the meeting made me realize that I had tapped into my area of passion. I couldn't wait for the next meeting to roll around on the calendar. On my drive home I called Chris to tell him how smoothly the event went. "I could do this kind of work every day for the rest of my life," I exclaimed.

Chapter 12
Third Time's a Charm

Chris and I were so excited to return to Dr. Halton's office for our post-op visit and the anatomy ultrasound to confirm our thoughts about the gender. Krista checked my cervix and we caught up on what was going on in each other's lives since my last visit. My cervix was over four centimeters long. The cerclage remained in place and our course could not have progressed more perfectly. We all breathed a sigh of relief and thanked God for the good news.

Krista applied warm gel to my stomach and proceeded with the scan. Instantly, we saw a very active baby on the flat screen monitor. Either the baby was practicing to be an acrobat, was aggravated at us for disturbing him or her, or was happy that we were peeking in to say hello. Regardless of the reason for all of the activity, we were happy to be spectators.

We saw a very strong heartbeat, the four-chambered heart, stomach, kidneys, and all of the other vital organs. She asked if we were ready to know the gender. "Absolutely," we replied.

Chris grabbed my hand as we fixed our eyes on the screen. The baby's long legs were crossed at the ankles. "That's got to be a little lady, look at how she's posing for us," I screamed!

"Well, you're right – it's a girl," she laughed, pointing out the genitalia.

Yes!!! We were right. Madison Noelle was coming into our home. I don't think we've ever felt that much excitement since our engagement or wedding. Tears rolled from my eyes, while I thanked God for giving us another precious little girl to love. Chris let go of my hand rather quickly and unexpectedly. I glanced at him just in time to see the glassy look in his eyes. Although the lights were out in the room, his tears lit up his eyes like bright stars in the sky. He was speechless! He rubbed his eyes quickly and asked when we should let our families know about Madison.

Krista finished the scan and gave us a CD with pictures from the ultrasound, and then we were escorted to a room to wait for our consult with Dr. Halton. We both pulled out our cell phones and called our families to share the news that little princess Madison would be coming into our home. Momma had all of my appointments written in her calendar and was anxiously waiting by the phone to celebrate with us. Everyone was elated to hear the news.

Dr. Halton entered the room, greeted us with a hug and congratulated me for having the longest cervix in the city. He was very pleased with the cerclage placement and my recovery. We were well on our way to a healthy full term delivery, but he still wanted to follow me closely. He reviewed the plan of care, which included alternating weekly appointments between his office and Dr. Laurel's office.

Initiation of weekly progesterone injections and biweekly cervical measurement checks with ultrasound were scheduled. If my award-worthy cervix were to shorten below two point five centimeters, I would immediately be placed on bed rest until delivery. Considering my history, bed rest was least likely to be in my future. All of the bases were covered and I knew to call his office if anything abnormal occurred.

Dr. Halton stressed to us that we could come in anytime for an ultrasound or just to listen to heart tones if we had any worries. His caring nature showed both personally and professionally. We checked out with Janice, scheduled the next two-week appointment and said our goodbyes.

Seemingly, my hope was increased and my faith was renewed. Each time we left the office with smiles and good news. We were so anxious to meet our daughter and adjust our lives to accommodate her. I hurried back to work and sent ultrasound pictures to my closest friends Lauren, Dominique, and Tenille. Countless emails followed with congratulations and their thoughts on which one of us Madison would look like.

Although the 3D ultrasound images were exceptional quality, I could not say who she resembled most. However, I could see that she was sleeping with her hands behind her head, which is the exact position that Chris slept in every night. She also refused to position her face appropriately for the sonographer to get a good picture. I concluded on the basis of those behaviors that Madison would act like her father, but would look like me.

It was easy to imagine ten years into the future, looking into the photo album and showing our daughter where she lived for the first nine months of her life. For the first time ever during pregnancy, I wanted to take belly pictures to document the changes to my body as I carried a miracle. Despite the over production of oil on my face, I felt exceptionally beautiful.

After church one Sunday, I convinced Chris to be the photographer and capture the first of many coming monthly photo shoots. I posed in the kitchen, on the couch, by the fireplace, outside, and anywhere else that seemed picturesque. Surprisingly, I enjoyed my impromptu shoot much more than I thought I would. After the session ended, I downloaded the pictures from the camera and posted them to my blog, which I had started several months before.

Charlie, the assistant at my dentist's office, shared stories with me about her cousin, Rebecca. She unsuccessfully tried for years to conceive a baby, but had no luck. Rebecca started a blog about her quest for motherhood and found that sharing her story was therapeutic. I started following her and with nearly each blog entry I nodded in agreement. Rebecca welcomed twins into the world and I was able to celebrate her strength and her growing family. Although our circumstances were different, our desire was the same. I identified with the longing to share our story and our love.

The new blog pictures revealed how proud I was. The smile on my face confirmed the happiness radiating in my heart and the sense of relief that was in my mind. The weight of worry and anxiety had been exchanged for peace, optimism, and excitement. My vision of building a family was coming closer into view, just as I knew it would.

Chris and I headed out for our weekly date night of dinner, window shopping, and walking downtown. He had choir rehearsal that Friday evening, so we opted for a Thursday date night instead. We stopped in several boutiques to look at all of the adorable clothes and decorations I had to have for Madison. I even warned him that the checkbook and debit cards would be over utilized within the coming weeks and months and he didn't seem to be concerned at all.

We chatted about how our lives would change when Madison arrived and how much we would both miss our Sunday afternoon naps. Regardless of how our lives were expected to change, we were ready and up for the challenge. I was certain that the joy before us was greater than the pain behind us. It was indeed the best of times.

Our date ended with a very active baby dancing inside of my belly. Chris firmly pressed his hand upon my stomach to feel the precious miracle that was dancing to the sound of his voice. He was amazed at how strong and forceful Madison's movements were. Chris ended the night with his usual ritual of singing the ABC's to her and kissed my belly. He prayed for our family and thanked God for His faithfulness shown to us, followed by a goodnight kiss for me.

The following Friday, we went about our normal day, but had to hurry home to get ready for choir rehearsal with Momma Dawkins. We were so happy to see our friends and they were just as happy to see the three of us. Our friend Millie gently scolded me for the wedge sandals I had on and reminded me that I needed to wear flat shoes. Following her instructions, I took off my sandals and gave them to Chris. He went to the car and returned with my flip flops.

I sat in the congregation and sang along with the group. Before I knew it, my eyes were closed and I was swaying back and forth to the rhythm of the melodious sounds. Something about the music had a euphoric way of touching my heart and bringing peace to my soul. I waited until there was a break between songs before finally getting up to go to the restroom. I didn't want to miss a minute of the rehearsal. I hurried to the restroom and quickly made my way back to my seat, just in time for the introduction of the next song. Within a few minutes, I had the urge to use the restroom again. *'My little Madison must have been rocking and swaying to the music just as I was and moved onto my bladder,'* I thought to myself.

Madison didn't know that I was determined to execute the same plan of rocking and swaying until the next musical break. I hoped the continued rocking and swaying would have the reverse effect on her and allow her to roll away from my bladder. The more I rocked, the greater the urge was to make my way to the bathroom. So I was forced to abandon my plan and quickly made my way to the restroom. There was so much pressure in my lower abdomen that it immediately made me sit down each time I tried to stand.

When I used the restroom I was very surprised by how little urine I actually produced. It was strange, because there was such an enormous urge to go. I sat on the toilet for a few minutes more in hopes that more urine would come and relieve the pressure I felt. So, I stared at the rose-colored wallpaper and read the scriptures in the well-decorated bathroom to focus. A few trickles came sporadically, but I never got the relief I wanted.

I wiped and inspected the toilet paper, which was my practice since December 2007, when my water broke with Destiny. The euphoric feeling that flooded my heart and soul vanished before my heart took the next beat. I saw a tan, mucous tinged string on the toilet paper and immediately knew it was my mucous plug. I closely inspected the mucous and wiped again and there was even more with the second round of wiping.

My heart raced, beads of sweat began to pour through my thick hair and down my neck. Panic had entered the restroom and hovered closely over me. I composed myself enough to go back into the sanctuary, but didn't want to cause a disturbance and needed to come up with a plan. I sat in my seat, rummaged through my purse for my keys and cell phone. A simple message to Maxine was quickly sent: "Call me when you get a chance. I think something is going on with my cervix."

Chris looked at me and mouthed, "Are you okay?"

I hesitated and shook my head "yes."

Maybe the lack of color on my face told him differently. I proceeded outside to call the after-hours line for my OB. As I sat in the car my trembling hands could barely dial the pager number. I entered my call back number as instructed and hoped for an expedited return call. Within minutes my phone rang. "Hello, this is Suzanna. How may I help you?"

I was relieved, simply by hearing the caring, compassionate voice that I knew all too well. Suzanna walked through the valley of death with us before and her presence illuminated our dark path. "Hey Suzanna, this is Tanika Dillard. I'm sorry to bother you, but I am a little concerned that I just passed my mucous plug."

"Oh sweet girl, I want you to come to the hospital right away. Given your history, I do not want to take any chances. How soon can you get here?"

"I can get there in thirty to forty minutes."

Maxine was returning my call, but I could not answer. She left a text message with instructions. *"Tee, go straight to L&D, stay off of your feet, and call me when you get settled at the hospital. I can come down there if you need me."*

Just as Suzanna was giving me instructions for where to report upon arrival, Chris was walking out of the door. He came to the passenger side window and said, "Babe, what is wrong?"

"We have to go to the hospital. I am pretty sure that I just passed my mucous plug, like I did with Briauna."

"Oh, God!" Chris sighed wanting full details. I gave him the abridged version and asked him to retrieve my purse from the sanctuary. He moved swiftly to get my things and to ask Momma Dawkins to pray for us as he had to leave due to an emergency. The singers began to bombard heaven before he even made it to the exit door.

Our drive to the hospital seemed to take an eternity, although he was going nearly ten miles per hour over the speed limit. The interstate kept growing, making our ride seem even longer. I reclined my seat and tried hard to whisper a prayer to heaven for divine intervention. Prayer was in my heart, but fear of the past echoed through my mind. Chris was quiet and simply put his sweaty palm on my stomach and left it there. I knew he was praying. Like me, he was fighting to silence the fear in his own mind in order to effectively pray.

We arrived at the hospital and went immediately to the fourth floor. I gave my name at the nurses' station and was escorted to room 437, just one door down from the previous room I had delivered in. I exchanged my denim maxi dress for a hospital gown and climbed into the bed.

There seemed to be a revolving door in my room. A very nice lab technician came in to draw my blood. I warned her that I was a hard stick and had very deep veins. I knew exactly where the good veins were and pointed her there. "You can try the vein right here in my left arm. It's deep, but it always works."

She swabbed the area with alcohol and firmly pressed to feel the vein. "Make a tight fist for me," she said as she tied a tourniquet tightly on my arm. "I'm just not feeling anything over here right now. Let me try the right arm for a better vein."

I extended my right arm and she began to poke, rub, and gently pat my arm in anticipation of seeing something. She turned my hand over and began to thump and pat again. "I feel a little vein here in your hand. I'm going to try it and see what happens."

The technician put on her gloves, swabbed my hand, and prepared the specimen tubes that needed to be filled. "Big stick," she said as the tiny needle seemed to pinch my skin. She wiggled it around and firmly pressed on my hand. There was no return. "I'm sorry; let me try your left arm again."

A nurse had come in to start my health history questionnaire and connect me to the monitors during the vein search. As the lab technician was shifting all of her supplies to the left side of the bed, the nurse connected me to two monitors. One monitor tracked Madison's heartbeat and the other monitored for contractions. The lab technician repeated all of the previous steps and lunged into my arm for the award-winning vein, which turned out to be a huge disappointment for both of us. "I am so sorry; I am not going to stick you anymore. Two attempts is my limit and then I call for backup."

"No need to apologize. I know I am a very difficult stick. It usually takes at least five tries before we have success."

As the technician used the call light to summons for help, the nurse proceeded with her questions. "Height and weight?"

"Five eleven and a lady never tells her weight," I said with a smile.

She never looked away from the computer screen and abruptly moved to the next question without appreciating nervous humor. "Any drug allergies?" she asked while tapping her fingers on the keyboard.

"None."

"Currently taking any medications?"

"Prenatal vitamins and progesterone injections."

"Number of pregnancies?"

I paused before answering. "Three."

"Number of live births?"

My heart and my voice dropped simultaneously, as I turned my head away from the nurse and gently answered, "None."

"Okay, that's all of the questions for now. We'll get your IV started in a few minutes." I absolutely despised all of the questioning. Surely, all of my information was tucked away in my medical record. Seemingly, the records would auto-populate the basic information and the other information could be gleaned from my office notes.

Debbie entered the room and stated that she was the head nurse coming to draw my labs. I apologized in advance for having to call in reinforcement. She proceeded to look at both arms as the lab technician showed her where she had previously stuck me. "Can you feel that?" The nurse doing my health assessment asked.

"Feel what? I honestly do not feel a thing."

"You are contracting and it looks to be pretty good, steady contractions at two to three minutes apart based on this printout. Let me go call Dr. C, who is on call this weekend for Dr. Laurel. She will have to give us orders on what we need to do."

I pressed my head as far into the pillow as I could. Chris placed his hand on my forehead as Debbie continued to stick me in hopes of vein access. His palms were just as sweaty as they were when we left the rehearsal. I could not even bring myself to look at him. All I could do was look at the ceiling tile and quietly say, "We are not losing another baby."

Debbie patted my leg ever so gently as if to offer her compassion for our unanticipated shocking news. "I am going to call down to anesthesia for help. I have tried several times and am not able to get a blood return. I apologize."

"It's okay, thank you."

The nurse returned with instructions from Dr. C. that I would be admitted for close monitoring during the night. Dr. C ordered IV antibiotics, fluids, and medication to stop the contractions. She would perform an ultrasound when she arrived to the floor. Although the hospital admission was unplanned, we were happy to be there rather than being at home worrying about what could happen. I encouraged Chris to head home and pack a bag for the both of us. He was adamant that he wasn't leaving my side and asked for pillows and a few blankets and settled in for the night.

Chris and I did not exchange words, but that didn't mean we didn't have anything to say. I was thinking how quickly things had changed for us in a matter of two short hours. I cradled Madison and told her that she would be okay.

Chris maneuvered his sleeper sofa as close to my bed as he could. His right hand was constantly in motion touching my forehead, rubbing my shoulder, or holding my hand. He didn't say much, but he was certainly talking to God and asking for Him to protect us.

We opted to wait until morning to contact our families. The day had nearly come to a close and we still didn't have concrete information on a plan. Dr. C. had not arrived to perform the ultrasound and we'd been in the hospital for nearly three hours. One of the nurses made a few calls and soon returned to our room with an ultrasound machine. Apologizing for the delay, she quickly set everything up and began to scan my stomach.

Madison was actively moving and her heart tones were great. My cerclage was still in place, but the nurse could see that I continued to have minor contractions, although I could not feel them. She gave me medicine to help me rest and more medication to stop the contractions. Both began to work immediately and I was sound asleep in no time.

Dr. Laurel arrived early Saturday morning to check on our progress. Thankfully, there were no contractions and everything appeared normal. As it turned out, I had a urinary tract infection, which they had already started antibiotics for. Dr. Laurel began to devise our plan of care for the duration of the pregnancy. I anticipated close monitoring and countless appointments in our future. Dr. Laurel prescribed complete bed rest for the remainder of the pregnancy, weekly home health monitoring, and weekly office visits with both him and Dr. Halton – he knew our history all too well.

My cervix had proven to be a bad actor, and he wasn't willing to leave anything to chance. He gave us the opportunity to ask questions, but we didn't have any as we knew the routine. He left the room to write out two prescriptions that I would need to stop the contractions. While he was away, Suzanna came in to review the discharge paperwork and remind us to call if we had symptoms of bleeding, contractions not relieved by medication, or fever.

Everything seemed all too familiar. It was indeed a *déjà vu* moment as I recalled the date. It had been precisely one year since I was in the same hospital, on the same floor giving birth to my sleeping daughter, Briauna. It was painful to remember her and the events surrounding her birth. It was equally painful to think that I would ever forget the events surrounding her birth. I simply wished that I could have enjoyed pregnancy with Madison more without being overcast with fear from Destiny's and Briauna's pregnancies. I'm certain that Jesus celebrates birthdays of little angels in heaven. I only wished there was an observation window so that we could see our precious girl, especially on her birthday.

We were discharged from the hospital with instructions to follow up with Dr. Halton on Tuesday for a repeat ultrasound and growth scan. Chris returned to work on Monday only after I insisted that there was no need for him to exhaust his vacation days babysitting me. I drove myself to the visit because I felt great and reassured him that everything was back to normal.

Unfortunately, I didn't get the news I expected. My cervix had shortened since my hospital discharge. Madison was positioned directly on my cervix, which was an additional eight ounces of pressure that I could not afford to have. The cerclage remained in place, however, and was maintaining my cervix and the pregnancy as expected. The ultrasound showed Madison to be happy and healthy. Despite hearing that my cervix had shortened, I was relieved to know everything else was well.

My strict bed rest orders remained in place. My home monitoring was set up to begin on Wednesday. I had absolutely no plans of doing anything except resting, getting up for bathroom breaks and shower. I informed Chris, Momma, and Lauren of the report from Dr. Halton. Without invitation from me or hesitation, Lauren called in the troops to help us out with our daily needs.

After Lauren left work, she arrived at our house with a care basket for us. It contained journals for me to write about my experience. It also had stickers, crossword puzzles, and an electronic game. She knew that I would need something to occupy my mind in the coming days, weeks, and months ahead. Lauren even created an online help registry for meals, grocery shopping, lawn care, and general help. She also came armed with paperwork and questions for Chris and I to answer – she had thought of everything.

As I answered, her numerous questions, I realized that I was simply and rapidly losing control. I had always been most proud of being Chris's wife, catering to and anticipating his needs. The bed rest adventure seemed to strip me of my most prized responsibility. The thought of not being able to make his lunch or kiss him goodbye as he left for work made my heart ache. I knew we would need a tremendous amount of help as we progressed forward. I had no choice but to embrace the kindness of others and accept the stillness that had been assigned to me. I cried constantly, thinking of the selfless acts and sacrifices that our friends and family made for us.

Though I was on bed rest, I had a major task before me since Chris's birthday was only six days away. Going out to dinner to celebrate was obviously out of the question, but bringing the celebration into our home was totally possible. I made phone calls to our family and friends and solicited help for bringing specific items to the birthday dinner on Sunday. Everyone was on board and excited to help make the celebration successful. The event had to come together flawlessly. Chris's last birthday occurred just a few days after Briauna's death. This year would be different!

My home health care nurse, Tammy, arrived Wednesday evening with a machine to monitor my contractions. She took her time explaining the device and how my contraction levels could be downloaded to their system. We started test-monitoring immediately to ensure that everything was set up properly. A quick call to the monitoring center showed that my data was being received and my uterus was "quiet" or not contracting.

I was instructed to monitor four times a day for at least thirty minutes. If I felt contractions at any other time, I was to monitor for an hour, drink plenty of water, and take a dose of the medicine to stop them. The process seemed simple enough and I felt comfortable doing it on my own.

Sunday came and I was so excited about hosting Chris's birthday dinner from his recliner, but felt a few vibrations prior to the guest's arrival. I had been on my feet getting minor things ready for the celebration. Perhaps the vibrations were my body's way of protesting any movement outside of the prescribed rest. So I promptly returned to the recliner with a large glass of water and two pills. I strapped the monitor around my stomach and rested as much as possible.

Nearly an hour later, I was still on the monitor contracting and it was time for the guests to arrive. I made a quick call to the monitoring center to inquire of my data reading. My uterus was anything but quiet. I was contracting every four to five minutes. I was instructed to stay on the monitor for another hour, drink plenty of water, elevate my feet, and take two more pills.

I wanted to hear something different. I had already done everything I was instructed to do without yielding favorable results. Despite my disappointment, I fully complied. Chris brought two pillows from the guest bed room to elevate my feet even more and made sure that my glass of water remained full.

Momma arrived and customary to her character had to be busy doing something, although there was nothing to do. Without my asking, she assumed the role of hostess just as I would have. Lauren picked up my contribution of chicken and a sheet cake from the deli/bakery at the local supermarket. Soon our house was filled with our families and close friends. The plan came together without a hitch. I felt so blessed and thankful to have such a great show of support for my dear husband. Chris seemed to enjoy the celebration and especially my mother-in-law's homemade banana pudding.

Of course, I maintained my position in the recliner throughout the party. I had to visit the restroom, but did not want to raise additional concern by moving frequently. I pushed my bladder to the maximum capacity before moving swiftly to the guest bathroom. I inspected the toilet paper, breathed a sigh of relief and returned to the recliner. "Are you okay?" Momma asked.

"Yes ma'am, I'm fine. I just had to use the restroom."

I strapped the monitor back around my stomach and within minutes I needed to use the restroom again. My mind started to wonder if something more was going on. I noticed the time and it had been nearly two hours since I made the call to the monitoring center and took another round of medicine. The contractions remained at the same pattern and intensity as they were hours before the celebration continued.

I made a conscious effort to remain in the conversations going on in the kitchen and in our family room, but my body was distracting me. The pulsating of my bladder caused thoughts of fear to creep into my mind. I could no longer engage in the conversation and made another swift exit to the restroom. This time I decided to sit there for a while. I figured if I retreated for ten minutes or so, I could completely clear my bladder and my thoughts.

The plan worked well. Within the first ten minutes, I was able to use the bathroom three times. Somehow, my bladder never felt empty and I still felt the urge to urinate. The pattern I was experiencing was all too familiar. I wiped and inspected the toilet paper multiple times, but there was nothing to sound an alarm. So I ended my restroom hiatus and rejoined the party guests. I had to respond to the question, "Are you okay?" several times within a very short time span.

"Yes, I'm fine, I just think Madison is lying on my bladder and I always feel like I need to go to the bathroom. I am fine though."

The time was nearly seven o'clock and our guests began to leave in clusters. I was unsure if they left simply because it was time to go or if they felt something more was going on that I wouldn't admit. Either way, I didn't protest their departure. By seven-twenty Lauren, Chris, and I were the only people remaining in our home. As soon as the last guest left, I was on my way to the restroom again.

The recurrent bladder-emptying started again followed by inspecting the toilet paper. Unfortunately, my worst fear was unfolding into a reality in the guest bathroom again. I hated that bathroom. It was filled with the beginning of bad memories. I saw the thick grey, pasta textured, thick, and stretchy mucous on the toilet paper. My head began to sweat and I was hot and clammy all over. I ripped off my underwear and walked across the hall to the guest room. "Babe, come here!!! Lauren, please come and bring my cell phone."

Chris scurried into the guest room and found me laying on the bed in the supine position with my legs gaped open as if ready for delivery. "What is it?" he asked.

I could barely catch my breath to explain what my eyes beheld. "I saw my mucous plug, just like I did with Briauna. We're going to have to go to the hospital. I feel a lot of pressure. Please look to see if you see anything."

I spread my legs further for his observation. Most of the color left his dark-skinned faced as he reported, "I see something white, but I don't know what that is."

Lauren stood at the entrance of the bedroom door and witnessed the unofficial exam. "Please look through my phone and call Dr. Halton and tell him what is going on," I requested as the adrenaline rushed through my body.

"Babe, can you bring me the mirror and a few towels?"

"Hello Dr. Halton, this is Lauren. I'm calling for Chris and Tanika Dillard. She wanted me to call you because she just went to the restroom and saw her mucous plug. She's lying on the bed now, but feels pressure and Chris saw something white between her legs."

Lauren was calm and professional and gave Dr. Halton the exact information he needed. Chris brought in the mirror and two turquoise beach towels. I positioned the mirror between my legs to observe exactly what he saw. I didn't know what it was, but I was sure it was not supposed to be seen yet. It was a grayish white contoured tube, resembling the umbilical cord, perhaps.

Lauren's voice trembled as she began to relay Dr. Halton's message. "Call 911 and have them transport you to the hospital and he will meet you there," she nervously explained.

"I think we would be okay to drive," I responded.

"Dr. Halton advised for ambulance transport," she repeated.

I quickly ended my rebuttal after continued inspection of the unidentified cord like object between my legs. Chris immediately called 911 and gave our address. I took the two oversized towels and positioned them under me as if I were putting on an adult diaper and gripped the sides of the towels so tight that my hands began to shake. I felt like my water was about to break and perhaps holding pressure to the area would prevent the inevitable from happening.

Lauren ended the call and her adrenaline took over. "Okay, what do you want me to pack in your hospital bag?"

I instructed her to our bedroom and told her where to find my toiletries, pajamas, and other items I would need. She quickly grabbed all of the necessary items and returned to the guest room for the next instructions. "Please take all of the food with you. We won't likely be here to eat it and it is just going to ruin," I told her.

Chris was moving hurriedly through the house to pack his bag and make sure all of the doors were locked. I suggested that he pack clothes for work in the event that Dr. Halton wanted to observe me for a few days. He had already taken a few days off after the prior hospital stay. I assumed it would be wise to reserve some vacation time for when Madison arrived. He could spend his days holding her rather than in the hospital with me.

The EMS arrived in front of our house and quickly came in. They started the triage process, asked too many questions, and applied oxygen to my nose. I positioned myself on the gurney while maintaining my grasp onto the towels. Chris and Lauren waited until I was in the ambulance before going to their cars. The medic pulled out supplies to get an IV started.

After twenty minutes and seven failed attempts later, I still did not have an IV and my blood pressure had to be off the chart. Surely, I was not dehydrated. I knew where my one good vein was and led him to it but he was unable to get a return. He insisted that he needed to start fluid on me before we could leave. I wanted to break out of the ambulance and run to get into the car with Chris. "Listen, I have been drinking all day because I've been contracting since early afternoon. I have had plenty of fluids. I am ready to go!!!"

He apologized and stated that he would let the hospital staff attempt the IV once we arrived. We finally left and headed for the hospital. The driver seemed to take his own precious time driving the ambulance. We were moving along at a non-emergent pace. I overheard the driver state the hospital address and I said, "No, we're going to the community hospital!!!"

The ambulance slowed to a crawl as he obtained correct information and informed the medic that we were rerouting. My anger and my blood pressure escalated to an all-time high. We finally arrived at the emergency room and I was transported to Labor and Delivery on the fourth floor. Dr. Halton was already at the nurse's desk awaiting my arrival.

My room quickly filled with a nurse, lab technician, Chris, and Dr. Halton. The lab technician drew blood and the nurse began her triage proceedings as Dr. Halton performed an internal examination. I didn't want to release the towels, which I had tightly held on to for over an hour. The exam was very quick as he could see my membranes bulging through the vaginal wall. He looked perplexed about the sudden turn of events. "I am so sorry. No one deserves to have children more than you two. We all want this so bad for the both of you."

Dr. Halton firmly rubbed Chris on the back and began to unveil his plan:

- Admit for observation.
- Initiate IV antibiotics and medication to stop the contractions.
- Maintain complete bed rest orders.
- Insert Foley catheter.
- Order sedative to help me relax.
- Perform ultrasound to check on baby.
- Apply heart monitor.
- Apply contraction monitor.

The nursing staff moved with haste to expedite the orders. By ten o'clock we were all settled in and ready for bed. I was so heartbroken that we had to be at the hospital and even more grieved that another black cloud would loom over Chris's birthday. We discussed his plan for work and decided that he would go report to work as long as I was stable throughout the night. He prayed over us and we drifted off to sleep. There were very few disturbances during the night, which allowed us both to get a good night's sleep. Chris woke early to reassess me before making the decision to go to work. I felt relaxed, my uterus was quiet, Madison was moving, and I felt at peace with him leaving.

In my most cheerful, morning, scratchy voice, I shouted, "Happy Birthday, Babe!" and extended my arms to hug him.

He smiled brightly and replied with an equally excited, morning voice, "Well, thank you." Then he leaned over to receive my hug and I held him as tightly as I did the turquoise towels the night before. Immediately, my eyes were filled with tears as I thought about how he must be feeling on his birthday, yet feeling the responsibility to work to provide for us despite the uncertainty of our situation. He was not concerned about his birthday; he was concerned that we would be okay.

As he prepared to leave he gave me instructions to call if anything changed. He confirmed his supervisor's number in my cell phone and told me he would call to check on me during his break times. After another long hug and more crying, he was on his way to work his ten-hour shift.

As soon as the door closed, I released the reservoir of tears that I had held since Sunday night. The bed linens proved to be strong enough to absorb the weight of my sobs. I needed to release my fears, my disappointment, and my frustrations with our attempts to build a family–and I needed to find some way to heal my heart that was breaking again.

My cell phone rang during my emotional meltdown. Chris hadn't even reached the highway and was calling to make sure I was okay. I sat up in the bed as an attempt to disguise my emotional state. "Why are you crying?" he asked.

There was an extended pause as I quickly thought of what was appropriate to say. "I'm fine, Babe. I just hate this, especially today."

We continued our conversation until he made it safely to work. After saying our goodbyes I drifted back off to sleep, which seemed most appropriate after a good cry. My eyes had been closed for less than half an hour before the nurses and lab technicians made their morning rounds. I dreamed of being at a five-star hotel and inserting a fancy, "Do Not Disturb" marker on the door. The reality was that I needed every bit of medical care and attention they could offer and sleep would have to wait until much later.

Shortly before eleven o'clock, I began to feel the unwanted contractions again. I immediately called for my nurse and told her what I felt. Dr. Laurel had written for me to have medicine to stop the contractions as needed. Within minutes, I had taken two small blue pills and anxiously waited for my uterus to become quiet.

As promised, Chris called from work on his lunch break for a status update. There wasn't much to update other than the contractions. Dr. Laurel had not made his rounds, so there was no change in the treatment plan. I heard the concern in Chris's voice and of course began to cry, but kept an upbeat voice to disguise the tears. My heart was simply heavy.

Momma entered the room and saw me lying on my side in Trendelenburg position in the bed with my head to the floor and feet elevated, silently weeping. She dropped her purse, sat beside me on the bed and began gently rubbing my back. "Has Dr. Laurel been in today?"

My tears got in the way of my words. I could only shake my head, "No."

She probed further to understand my reasoning for crying. Despite my best efforts, I could not speak a word. Just as any other good mother would, she asked, "Is there anything I can do?"

I shook my head "no" again. I could hear the agony in her voice and how it pained her to see me in such an emotional state. Although she didn't ask any more questions, I knew she was talking to God about our situation. She continued to rub my forehead and back until the lullaby of my sobbing calmed me to sleep.

Dr. Laurel made his rounds shortly after four o'clock. I was glad to see him and anticipated that he would have an expert opinion and plan for my emergent care. As he began to disclose his plan, I knew my anticipated response wasn't going to happen as I imagined. There wasn't a master plan in the works. In fact, Dr. Laurel suggested that I just relax and hope for the best. The "best" in his opinion would be to hold on to the pregnancy for as long as possible. Our target was until the age of viability at twenty-eight weeks, which meant nine weeks of hospitalizations and/or bed rest. I was willing to do absolutely anything to bring our daughter home.

Dr. Laurel did not see the benefit of me continuing to lie in Trendelenburg position and suggested that I make myself comfortable, but continue the strict bed rest orders. Although I respected his medical advice, I opted to continue the Trendelenburg position and hope that gravity would work with me to suction the bulging bag of water and membranes into its rightful place. I couldn't give up so easily. I was willing to keep my head pressed upon the headboard of the hospital bed for as long as necessary.

Watching the clock move closer to five o'clock, I knew Chris would be getting off work and calling me for an update. I needed to be happy and focus all of my attention and energy into celebrating him. Sadly, I was empty and had nothing to offer other than tears and a targeted pregnancy goal of twenty-eight weeks. Based on the persistent contractions, I wasn't certain that my body was as determined to continue the pregnancy as I was.

Chris called immediately after getting into his car. We engaged in a brief conversation about his day and I managed to maintain a happy tone. I told him that we would discuss Dr. Laurel's report once he arrived. My heart raced as I ended the phone call. My sweaty palm gripped the side of the bedrail as I anticipated seeing his face. A steady stream of tears silently dripped onto my pillow. I heard his footsteps in the hallway and he entered the room with a boisterous, "Hey Babe!"

Those few seconds held the perfect dichotomy of joy and pain. I lifted my head off the pillow as he bent over to kiss my face. "Babe, you are burning up. Do you have a fever? What is wrong?"

Actually, I felt fine and didn't even notice that I had a fever. I repeated all of the information from Dr. Laurel and told Chris that we needed to pray for a miracle and believe that we could continue the pregnancy until the twenty-eighth week. I failed to ask Dr. Laurel if I would need to be inpatient for the duration of the pregnancy or if I would be closely followed as an outpatient. I wanted the peace of mind that accompanied the watchful eye of the medical professionals. However, I could not fathom being in the hospital bed alone or Chris sleeping in our house alone. While I was completely willing to cooperate with any plan that was established, I did not have to like it.

We held hands tightly and opted not to speak. Each stroke of his hand caressing mine seemed to send a message of, "I love you, I am here with you, and I am hurting also." His warm, strong hand reminded me that we were on this journey of building a family together. Just being together, especially during this time of uncertainty, was exactly what we both needed.

Our godparents, the Dawkins, called and wanted to come visit us if we were up to company. Their timing could not have been more perfect. Minutes prior, I had asked Chris to play the CD that "Momma Dawkins" (as we affectionately called her) had recorded a couple of years prior. All of the songs on the CD were based from the sacred scriptures that we reflected on for strength. I thought it best that we created an atmosphere for miracles right in our hospital room. Momma and Pop Dawkins came to check on us, but they really had a divine assignment to come and encourage our hearts.

Their brief yet impactful visit was God-inspired and refreshing to our souls. Momma Dawkins saw the pain on my face and encouraged me. Pop Dawkins saw the mental heaviness Chris carried and encouraged him. They let us know that it was okay for us to be supported by others and have others pray for us even when we could not find the strength or the words to do so ourselves. Momma Dawkins gently laid her hand upon my fevered head and summoned the aid of our God to hear her supplications. Her prayers stirred my faith to believe on a greater level. Her tenacity in prayer reminded me of Grandma. There was no way that God wouldn't turn His ear to Momma Dawkins' prayer. In fact, I was fairly certain that her prayers expedited the miracle that we all waited for.

In the same manner, Pop Dawkins embraced Chris and prayed fervently, specifically for him. He knew the weight Chris silently carried and the concern that was upon his heart. Pop Dawkins' voice resonated like an army of warriors as he pleaded for peace and strength for Chris. Faith abounded in our room. The atmosphere conducive for miracles that we wanted had been established.

Chris was exhausted and I could see it all over his face. I encouraged him to go home, take a hot shower, and have a good sleep in our bed rather than have another night on the uncomfortable hospital recliner. He persistently refused to leave, while I forcefully protested him staying. I made my argument that he needed a good night of sleep after an eventful night previously and having worked a long ten hour shift. I assured him that I would be fine and would immediately call him if anything changed. He reluctantly agreed and left me with plenty of kisses, a belly rub for Madison, and a prayer that God's perfect will would be accomplished in our lives.

My protector hated to leave and I hated to see him walk out of the door. I wiped away the tears, grabbed my laptop, and played Momma Dawkins' CD to allow the peace that filled our room just hours before to sweep over my soul once more. Music proved to be the perfect remedy. Chris called when he arrived home and I was jolted from my sleep by the sound of the phone. We said our goodnights and both prepared to bring the long day to a close.

I closed my eyes with the anticipation of quickly drifting back to sleep. Though I was a bit uncomfortable, I repositioned myself in the bed. I simply could not get comfortable, but couldn't pinpoint the source of my discomfort. I closed my eyes and hummed along to the music in hopes of drifting to sleep.

Frustrated by my insomnia, I pressed the call light for my nurse Crystal to bring me some medicine to help me sleep. While she was in the room she checked my vitals, assessed my pain, and asked if she could get anything else for me. She elevated my feet onto two pillows and gave me another pillow to place between my legs in an effort to get comfortable. It worked! I finally was comfortable and sleepy, perhaps partially due to the medicine.

I woke up shortly before midnight to go the restroom, and then remembered that I had a foley in place and could not get out of bed. I rolled over on my back and heard what sounded like a balloon being popped. My water broke! My heart raced as I felt the soaked sheets. "I need my nurse please!!!" I yelled as I pressed the call light.

Crystal entered the room right away. "I am pretty sure my water just broke," I explained.

She checked me and confirmed my suspicion to be true. What a way to end Chris's birthday. "Let me call Dr.

Laurel to see what he wants to do. I will be back as quickly as I can and I'll bring some new bed linens."

I dialed the first three digits of Chris's number and immediately hung the phone up. I wavered between calling him, waiting until I knew the plan from Dr. Laurel, or waiting until morning, but I had promised I would call him if anything changed. Chris quickly answered on the second ring. "Babe, my water just broke," I cried.

I heard him maneuver around in bed to sit up. "What happened?" he asked.

"I'm not sure why it happened, but my water broke and Crystal is calling Dr. Laurel now."

"Oh no, I am on my way. Are you okay?"

Dr. Laurel added an additional IV antibiotic and would be in to see me when he made his morning rounds. Clearly, I could recline the bed and sleep in any position I wanted. The efforts to relieve cervical pressure were no longer needed. I had lost this round of the fight.

Chris quickly arrived to my room and was greeted with open sobbing. He held me tightly until I could find the words to say. "I just cannot understand why this would happen to us again." I knew he did not have the answer and I did not expect him to. He likely had the same questions as I had.

Dr. Laurel arrived early Tuesday morning. His tone was somber and so was the news he delivered. Based on his medical knowledge, he concluded that my body would likely begin active labor at any time. My blood work showed evidence that my white blood count was elevated, which was a sign of infection. I was taken back to the operating room to have the failed cerclage removed. Despite hopes of prolonging the pregnancy until twenty eight weeks, the reality was delivery was imminent.

My vitals and Madison's heart tones were checked every four hours. I welcomed the close monitoring of Madison's, since I could not feel her moving any more after the water broke. We heard a very strong heartbeat and fetal movement with each observation, for which Chris and I breathed a sigh of relief.

By Thursday morning, my body had not begun to actively labor. Dr. Laurel and the ethics committee at the hospital gave permission for medicine to induce labor. I saw the distress and weariness on my husband's face and felt helpless. He filtered all of the phone calls and gave the grim report to everyone that needed details. There were always more questions asked of him than he could answer. He exuded strength despite the pain in his heart. The tone of his voice lowered with each subsequent call. "Babe, what are you feeling? Please talk about whatever is on your mind and do not feel like you have to be strong for me," I assured him.

"I'm okay," he quietly responded.

I knew him better than he had given me credit. I knew he was hurting. When he stepped out of the room to answer a call, I quickly phoned my daddy. I explained the latest developments. "Daddy, can you come to the hospital to be with Chris? He's hurting and no one seems to realize just how much. I cannot get through to him."

The nursing staff, my doctors, and my family were very supportive, but Chris needed another man to just be there for him and give him the permission to cry without questioning his manhood. At my request, Momma patiently waited in the lobby when Daddy came to see about him. Daddy was a quiet, yet powerful presence in the room. He didn't overwhelm Chris with questions or engage us in mindless chatter. He encouraged us in our faith. "I cannot imagine the pain that either of you feel. I am sure that you both have a thousand emotions that you are feeling now. Just allow yourself to feel them and don't think about anything else."

Our nurse, Allison explained that she would place the two white pills on my cervix. The pills would soften my cervix and that would begin the induction process. I signed a medical consent and the procedure could begin whenever we gave Allison the green light. Daddy and Chris were the only ones in the room. "Would you like for anyone to step out before I place this on your cervix?" she asked. I was completely agreeable to having the man who loved me all of my life and the man who conceived Madison in love stay in the room.

Allison's voice trembled when she asked me to verify my date of birth as she scanned the barcode of the medicine into the computer. I looked over at her and saw a steady stream of tears run down her red face. She knew the finality of the moment before her.

Chris fell to his knees beside my bed and began to openly weep as he placed his trembling hands upon Madison and me. He felt helpless and powerless in saving Madison's life. The thought of her struggling to survive in my womb without fluid for her lungs proved to be too much of a burden for him to accept.

For the first time in two and a half years, the emotional fort Chris had built crumbled. I had never witnessed him shed a tear about Destiny or Briauna. I knew Chris cried, but he refused to let me see him in that state. Our roles had reversed and I was able to comfort him.

I rubbed his head and back as he continued to kneel beside the bed. "It's okay, Babe. We will get through this."

My sincere words were no match for the pain that raged inside of his heart. I did, however, find pleasure in comforting him. I had longed for the moment when we could share tears together. I had never heard such heartfelt anguish come from a grieving father, especially my husband. I didn't try to silence him. "Babe, take all of the time you need to talk to her. There is no rush."

His gentle, heartfelt words to Madison would have warmed the coldest of hearts. "Oh, my little baby girl, I am so sorry you are fighting for your life in there. I would do anything to save you. Anything!!! God, please help us."

He visualized Madison's struggle inside of the darkest, driest chamber of my unreliable womb. The mental picture must have included flashbacks of Destiny and Briauna who struggled just as Madison was at the moment. His weeping turned into intense lamenting and I could no longer decipher his words other than a tearful refrain of, "I'm so sorry."

Although there was absolutely nothing that he could have done to prevent our calamity, he felt the responsibility as a good father to protect his child. Our dream of building a family was turning into another nightmare and breaking both of our fragile hearts again.

Chris wiped his tears with the white hospital blanket on my bed. After a long pause he lifted his glossy, red eyes and spoke, "I'm sorry. You can go ahead now," he told the nurse in a soft and solemn voice. His strong, squared shoulders curved inward as he surrendered to the pain within his heart.

Allison knelt down on the left side of my bed with tears still in her eyes. She reassured us as she rubbed Chris on the hand, "there is nothing to be sorry about. I do not have to place the medicine until you both are completely ready."

Our eyes met and we both nodded in agreement that it was time to proceed. We would never be ready had the choice been left to us, but we knew we had to move forward if we didn't want to jeopardize my life. "I need to recline your bed all of the way back and then we can get started," Allison said pressing the button to adjust the bed and dropping the bed rail to be as close to me as possible.

"Now, place your knees in the air. I will be as gentle as possible," Allison instructed.

Our hearts synchronized as one loud, fast beating drum. Our hands were gripped tightly as the pills were applied to my cervix. I looked at the ceiling tile as if I were looking into heaven and silently asked for a miracle. Chris rested his lips on my hand and closed his eyes, but did not utter a word. "I'm all done," Allison said empathetically. "I need to check your vitals and Madison's heart tones before I go."

Chris quickly stood from kneeling by my bedside. "I am going outside. I can't hear her struggling anymore," and headed for the door with my Daddy following him.

The uncertainty of the moment made me nauseous. I knew what I wanted to hear, but I also knew the reality of not hearing a heartbeat. Allison hooked me up to the monitor and we both waited with bated breath. "There it is! She's fine – 154 beats per minute!" Allison proclaimed.

From what we could tell, Madison was not in any immediate distress. I exhaled with a sigh of relief, "Thank you Lord."

I called Momma to give her an update. She was on her way back to the room and arrived just in time for the administration of the epidural. "Hi, I'm Anna, I've come to make you comfortable," the anesthesiologist said as she adjusted her blue cap.

"Thank you."

"I'm going to wash your back off three times and locate a space in your lower back for the injection. This should only take a few minutes. Do you have any questions for me?"

"No, I understand."

Allison stood in front of me and I tightly squeezed her hands as the needle was inserted. The process was quick and painless. "Okay, we're all done – best of luck to you," Anna said as she exited the room.

I lay in the bed in silence as my body went numb from my waist to my toes. I knew that I would never feel Madison's tiny body inside of me again for sure now. I cradled my arms around my stomach, closed my eyes and drifted off to sleep. It seemed like I was only asleep for a few minutes, but I had actually been asleep for two hours. "Hey again, I'm sorry to wake you, but I wanted to say goodbye before I left," Allison said.

"My goodness, it's almost seven o'clock already?" I said while stretching.

"Yes, and you've been sleeping good, I just wanted to let you and Chris know that you are in my prayers and so is little Miss Madison. You guys have been through so much. I just wanted you to know I'll be thinking of each of you tonight." Allison did not hold back the tears and neither did I.

"Gina will be your nurse for tonight. Do not hesitate to call her. Now, can I get anything for either of you before I go?"

"I don't need anything, but I'm sure Chris could likely use some coffee. Momma, do you want anything?"

"I'll just have water please, if you don't mind."

Allison returned to the room quickly with the drinks and gave us all a hug before heading home to her family. By ten o'clock in the evening, I started feeling the first signs of discomfort. Gina did a quick internal exam and reported that I had only dilated one centimeter since the induction started six hours previously. I was very hopeful that I had made significant progress and was closer to delivery. "Gina, how often can I press this button for more medicine? I'm starting to feel pretty crampy."

"You can press the button any time you feel pain. If you happen to exceed the internal limit, nothing will be dispensed, so do not be afraid to click the button." Without hesitation, I pressed the magic button and held it for a few seconds for good measure.

Chris pulled his chair closer so that there wasn't an inch of space between the two of us. Several times an hour, he'd ask, "How are you feeling now?"

I didn't want to complain, but I was in pain. My legs were numb and they felt like they weighed a thousand pounds each. I could not move to turn over or adjust to get more comfortable. I became more miserable by the minute. My patience had grown thin and I wanted this slow moving emotional rollercoaster to end. The hands on the clock moved passed the midnight hour, then past the one o'clock hour, then past the two o'clock hour. I had only dilated to four centimeters. My body had exerted far beyond its mental and physical limits. "I cannot do this for another minute! I want this to be over!!!"

Chris's eyes were red from exhaustion and his emotions. "Babe, you don't have to do this ever again. I just can't stand to see you in this type of pain."

BUILDING A FAMILY BREAKS MY HEART

There was so much relief knowing I would never be expected to labor again. However, in the same moment, I realized that although I did not want the pain, I still wanted to have children. "What are we going to do about building a family?" I inquired.

"We can adopt or something, but I just don't want you to go through this ever again."

That was a loaded discussion that would have to be tabled until another day when the pain of childbirth didn't cloud my rational thinking. I had to bring myself back to the task at hand, which was birthing Madison. I felt a strong urge to use the bathroom. I quickly pressed the call light and spoke with the operator. "May I help you?"

"Yes, could you ask my nurse to come in please?"

"Can she bring you anything?" the operator asked.

"No, I just need to get up to use the bathroom. I feel a lot of pressure."

"I'll send her in right away."

As promised, Gina entered the room and grabbed two purple gloves from the box on the wall. "Let me check you before you get up." She reclined my head and instructed me to relax as she delicately performed an internal check. "Do not push; whatever you do. I need to get Dr. Laurel here because it's time."

Gina moved to the side of my bed and pressed the call light, "Page Dr. Laurel to room 432 STAT!" She elevated my bed for the birthing position, grabbed several hospital blankets from the supply closet and put on a yellow sterile gown. "Hold on Hun! He should be here any minute now."

"I can't! I feel so much pressure. I have to push!"

I bit my bottom lip and squeezed Chris's right hand with intensity in an effort to minimize some of the pain, but it didn't work. Momma, Chris and I were silent as the nursing supervisor and others rushed in to help Gina with the impending delivery. Our hearts beat, thud thud, thud thud, in unison as we braced ourselves for Madison's arrival. My body was ready to set her free, but my heart would never be ready. "I feel her coming!!!"

125

"Dr. Laurel is only three minutes away," Gina announced. "Just hold on!"

"I have to push!!! I'm not waiting any longer!!!"

Momma gathered from my tone that things were about to take a major shift. She ran into the bathroom and pulled the door behind her, leaving only a small space open. She had been present to witness the births of Destiny and Briauna, but she could not bear to see another granddaughter come into the world silently. I took a glance through the small crack in the door. Momma was leaning over the sink with tissues to her face crying out in prayer for a miracle.

Gina, the nursing supervisor, and nearly five additional support staff stood silently in the room waiting for the arrival of Dr. Laurel or Madison. Whichever person came first, they were prepared to act. Everyone had on blue sterile masks and purple gloves. I could no longer contain the life inside of me. I gripped the left bed rail and Chris's right hand. Gina instructed me, "Put your chin to your chest and push."

I pushed and felt increased pressure and pain. I leaned up in the bed, pushed again and immediately thrust my back against my pillow. As quickly as a rollercoaster takes off for a thrill ride, Madison was quickly ejected from my body. "3:10 A.M," said the nurse supervisor.

"Cord around neck times two," Gina said.

"Oh no, the cord was around her neck?!!!" I screamed with my arms outstretched to receive our precious daughter as Gina worked to untangle and cut the umbilical cord.

The nurse supervisor said, "It's better that it happened now than for this to have happened later."

There was nothing about her statement that brought me comfort. Was Madison's death really better at nineteen weeks gestation than having the same type of loss at twenty nine weeks? Why was time significant with her loss I wondered for only half of a second? I had other things to do rather than try to decipher well-meaning comments.

I saw the helplessness in the tears that filled Chris's eyes. He leaned over the bed to kiss my forehead. I could hear

Momma loudly weeping in the bathroom. "Have mercy Lord. Have mercy."

Dr. Laurel burst in the door just as Gina was placing Madison in my hands. "Here she is."

I did not count her fingers or toes. I gently placed her tiny unclothed body against my chest. I closed my eyes to minimize the tears that immediately formed the very second I touched her. The room was silent with the exception of tearful echoes from the bathroom. There were no cheers, applause, or congratulations. The entire medical team simply gazed at us. Surely, we were not the first family to experience a pregnancy loss in the hospital. However, we could very well have been the first family to have experienced three losses there.

Tears fell from my face and onto Madison's tiny head. After holding her for only a few seconds, I heard her gasp for breath. "Did you hear that?" I asked Chris.

"Did she just breathe?" he asked as a smile appeared on his face.

"She's alive, Momma!!! She's alive!!!" I yelled.

Momma swung the door open and bolted into the room. Dr. Laurel didn't move closer to rescue the miracle in my hands. The medical support team in their gloves and sterile masks stood frozen in time. "Do something!!! She's alive!!!" I demanded.

Dr. Laurel quietly explained, "The breathing that you see is likely excess calories she's burning off. However, if we were to evaluate her for brain activity, we would not find anything. At this gestational age, it is not hospital policy to initiate heroic measures to save her life."

"What?!!! Can you at least give her some oxygen since she is breathing on her own?" I inquired.

Dr. Laurel communicated "no" by shaking his head.

"Can we transfer to another hospital that will help save her? Somebody has to do something!" I asked in despair.

The answer was, apologetically, "no" again. "She will likely only sustain these breathes for a few minutes more.

Just try to make the most out of the time you have remaining with her," he said.

Anger came upon me like hot lava erupting from a volcano as a host of non-assisting medical professionals stood watch by my bedside waiting for death to come. Their prolonged stay proved to be futile after the first twenty-five minutes. We could see Madison's rapid heartbeat through her translucent skin. "Get out! Everybody, get out!!!" I screamed as the medical staff continued to gaze at us with eyes of pity, folded hands and amazement.

The precious moments we had with Madison needed to be spent privately rather than with an audience of spectators. In silence, the staff scurried out of the room. "We'll be right outside if you need us. I'll need to weigh her and take her measurements, but we can do that later," Gina said.

Hot tears raced down my face as the room cleared. I was not crying because of Madison's fate. I was crying because her life did not seem valuable enough to salvage. Chris, Momma, and I watched Madison's chest rise and fall in amazement. By the knowledge of the professionals, the lungs of a nineteen week old baby were too immature to function independently for more than several minutes. Madison was breaking records and changing the statistics for the good. If no one was going to fight for her life, she was determined to fight for her own and we were going to be there with her every breath of the way.

Madison was a warrior! There were times when her breathing would decelerate and get a little shallow. We could see her heart beating only several times a minute and it looked like the end was near. However, we were not giving up on the tenacious miracle that we loved. I would pull her closer to me, breathe on her, and whisper, "Live Madison, live!" and she quickly responded by catching her breath and her heart rate would increase back to normal.

By six o'clock that morning, Chaplain Cynthia had arrived to work and headed straight for our room to meet Madison. She brought in with her a beautiful handmade pink, smocked gown for her. She started making the gown as soon as she found out that we were pregnant with a daughter. The gown was delicate soft linen with white eyelets along the hem. The precise stitching and detail of the dress confirmed that it was made with love. Madison's small eight ounce body was much too little to wear the dress. However, I envisioned her being a healthy eight pound girl wearing the gown.

Cynthia held Madison and her eyes filled with tears. She had been such an integral part of our support system since Briauna's birth. Cynthia was emotionally vested in the pregnancy. She kept track of my doctor's appointments and would call to check on Chris and me often. She wanted us to have a good outcome just as much as we did. We had become family.

News of Madison's arrival spread quickly. Our phones were constantly ringing from our friends and family as they offered their congratulations, support, and prayers. Momma filtered the calls so Chris and I could focus all of our time and attention on our precious daughter.

Tina came directly from her third shift job to meet her newest niece. "Oh, she's so tiny," she whispered as Momma carefully placed Madison in her arms. I felt so proud seeing my family fill Madison's life with love. Tina rocked Madison and commented about how much she looked like Chris.

After each ultrasound with Dr. Halton, we had looked closely at the details of the digital images that we were given. We concluded that Madison would look like me based on her long extremities and would act like Chris based on her camera shyness. We, in fact, were very wrong. Madison did have long legs, long feet, and long fingers, but she had all of Chris's features. She had his round nose, mouth, the line in his forehead and skin color. I was hopeful that she would inherit at least one of my dimples, but she didn't.

Shortly after seven o'clock, Suzanna came to our room. She had already received the report from our night shift nurse. "How are y'all doing?" she asked as she washed her hands. She then took a seat on my bed and reached for

Madison from Tina. "My goodness, I am holding a miracle," she said with her soft voice.

"I've been doing this kind of work for a long time and nineteen-week-old babies just do not make it as long as Madison has. She is a fighter and y'all should be so proud."

"We are amazed that she is still alive. The staff thought she'd only live for a few minutes," I said.

Suzanna's eyes were fixed upon Madison. She closely watched her breathing and stroked her soft, bald head. "Who did she get this chin dimple from?" she asked with a smile.

I leaned forward in the bed to see exactly what she was pointing to. I too, had looked at seemingly every inch of her tiny body and did not see a dimple anywhere. To my surprise, there was indeed a dimple in her chin, identical to the dimple Chris has. "Babe, wake up! You have to see this. Madison has your dimple in her chin."

Chris awakened from his deep sleep in the recliner with a bear like stretch. "What happened?" he asked.

"Nothing happened; I just want you to see that Madison has your dimple in her chin." He smiled as he leaned closer in to see and immediately reached for the camera to capture more pictures and a video. He was so proud of his daughter and even more proud that she looked just like him.

Suzanna left to check on her other patients, but told us to call the nurses' station if we needed anything. Tina also left to go home for a few hours of sleep. She was exhausted after ten hours of working and visiting with us. She carefully lifted Madison close to her cheek and paused in search of the appropriate words to say. Her eyes looked like glass as she tried to hold back the tears that filled her eyes. "Auntie loves you!" she said passionately as her tears touched the purple blanket. She took another good look at Madison, signed heavily, and placed her in my arms. "Do y'all need anything?" Tina asked as she wiped her face.

"No honey, we are fine. Thank you for coming. I hope you go home and get some rest," I said.

"I'll try. Just call and let me know how she's doing or if y'all need anything," she said as we hugged goodbye.

Tina opened the door to exit the room, but froze in her tracks with one foot in the hallway and one in the room. She looked back over her shoulder into the room while biting her bottom lip in an effort not to burst into tears. She did not say a word with her mouth, but her tear filled eyes showed the message of her heart. "I... I love ya'll," she said in a quiet tone as she turned and quickly closed the door.

We were physically and emotionally exhausted. Chris was in the recliner snoring and Momma was beside me struggling to keep her eyes opened. I placed Madison on my chest, reclined the bed and hummed sweet lullabies to her until I drifted off into a conscious sleep. Every few minutes I would jolt myself awake to ensure that death had not snatched her away from us.

Cynthia returned to the room to check on us again. "I just wanted to bring something for Madison. I thought you might like the opportunity to dress her since the pink gown is too big."

Cynthia had found a lavender and white gown that had been donated to the hospital. It was no bigger than a handkerchief, but it was the perfect size for Madison. "Oh, absolutely! I would love to dress her," I said.

Momma stood to her feet and was excited to help dress her "Angel Girl." I unwrapped her blanket and put the dress on her as gently as I could. I took my time dressing her, because I did not know if I would ever have the opportunity to do so again. Momma tied the two lavender ribbons to close the back of the gown. "No, let me tie it again. This bow needs to be perfect."

"Momma, it's okay. It looks fine to me," I said.

"No, I have to redo it for my Angel Girl. It has to be right."

I immediately realized that Momma's actions were directly related to the thought I had as I dressed Madison. Perhaps this was the only time she would get to dress her granddaughter and she wanted everything to be flawless. I understood completely and smiled as Momma meticulously tied the perfect bow.

Ideally, our daughter would have been vibrant, with jet black, silky hair that I could adorn with beautiful handmade barrettes and headbands. She would have several couture dresses with matching socks, monogrammed keepsakes, jewelry, and props for her professional newborn photo session. I was ill-prepared. Unfortunately, it was nothing like I fantasized. I hadn't purchased anything because I honestly thought we would have more time. I also thought there would always be subsequent photo sessions and each one would be more glamorous than the first. I was wrong. Time was not on our side.

After Madison was properly dressed, the second round of her photo shoot began. I was the photographer and Momma was my assistant. I captured pictures of her tiny feet and hands, her smocked gown and pictures of Momma holding her. It was almost perfect except for the obvious. "Is she still breathing?" Momma asked.

"I think so. I've noticed that she's taking much longer breaths now and her heart rate has slowed down, but it's still beating. Maybe we wore her out with all of the pictures."

"Maybe we should just wrap her back up and make her comfortable for a little while," Momma suggested.

I swaddled Madison and laid her on my chest and gently cupped her tiny body with my hands. It was there, upon my chest that I began to prepare her for the journey ahead of her. "You get to go see your great-grandmas and your sisters Destiny and Briauna soon, precious girl. They are all going to love you so much. They will take good care of you. Don't be afraid, I'll hold you until you get to Grandma's house. Daddy and I will miss you, just as we miss your sisters, but we will always think of you and our love for you will never end."

I didn't want Madison to know that I was crying. I waited a few minutes before continuing my conversation to her. After I had dried my tears and wiped off the excess tears from her lavender blanket, I lifted her close to my face to give her the final instructions. "I know you are so young and this may be a lot for you to remember. Can you do a special favor for Mommy please, precious girl?"

My heart raced as I prepared to ask Madison to fulfill such an enormous task. "Please take all of these kisses to Destiny and Briauna and tell them that we love them." I placed countless kisses upon her head, but I knew that it would never be enough to last all three of our daughters for a lifetime. However, I knew I might never have the opportunity to send a special delivery to Heaven again, so I was committed to making this delivery unforgettable.

After the kisses I returned Madison to the safety of my chest and softly sang every lullaby that I had planned to sing to her when we took her home. I was certain that she shared our love for music. I couldn't think of a better gift to give her than melodies straight from my heart. I pulled back the lavender blanket to check on her, closely watching her heart pulsate through her transparent skin. Her chest did not move and the faint beating had ceased. I stroked her cheek in an effort to get her to respond, but she did not. I wrapped my hand around hers and gently stroked it. "You're okay, precious girl. Grandma will find you soon."

Madison had slipped away upon the melodies of my heart and was held by the Father in Heaven. Her passing was peaceful, pure, and reminiscent of Grandma's transition to her new home. "Babe, wake up," I whispered.

"Do you need something?" Momma asked from her seat beside my bed.

"No ma'am, I'm fine. I think she just left us."

"She what?" Chris inquired as he woke up with a bear-like yawn again.

"She's gone, Babe."

He stood to his feet and came to the bedside where he leaned in to see for himself that she had indeed taken her final breaths and had made her entrance into her new, forever home. Chris released a heavy sigh and shook his head. Although we were told that her death was certain, when it actually happened there were no words to describe the finality or the despair of the moment. He stood in silence and looked at his beloved daughter with a heartbroken look all over his face.

Momma cried silent tears, but smiled as she stood between us. "Are you okay, Son?" she asked as she rubbed his back in an effort to comfort him.

"Yes ma'am, I'm fine. I'm just thankful that she lived as long as she did. I'll go find Suzanna and Cynthia to let them know."

While we could have pressed the call light and called for Suzanna, I knew Chris needed a reason to step out of the room. "Okay Babe, take your time. If you are ready to let them come get her, they can now."

"Alright, I'll tell them, but they are going to bring her back right?" he asked.

"Yes, they just need to get her weight and footprints for the official paperwork and then she can come back."

"Oh, okay, that will be fine."

Suzanna came within a few minutes to get Madison and to see if we needed her to bring anything for us. "This sweet girl has amazed everyone on this floor. I am so thankful that you all had this time with her," she said with a smile as she carefully placed Madison in a small brown basket.

"I know, Suzanna. God must have known that we needed a new experience and let her live for the past nine hours. I am thankful also."

"Is it okay if I take her with me for a little while? I will bring her back as soon as I'm done. It will probably take me about thirty minutes," she said.

"Yes, that's perfectly fine. I'm not going anywhere."

I used the time to get out of the bed, stretch my legs, and shower. My five-month belly bump had already begun to deflate. I didn't have the radiant postpartum glow that I'd seen on so many women in the past. I did not have time to dwell on my outer appearance, because I needed to hurry and get back to the room to receive Madison from Suzanna. I was racing against the clock to get done in time, and I felt like a brand new woman after getting out of the shower.

My eyes were fixed on the clock in anticipation of Madison's return. After forty-five minutes, she was not back and neither was Chris. I knew Madison was in good hands, but I started to worry about my husband. I hesitated before slowly dialing his cell phone number and tried to rehearse the reason for my call. Surprisingly, the phone was forwarded directly to voice mail. There was no need to leave a message.

After an hour and a half Chris returned to the room. I didn't ask any questions regarding his whereabouts. He took the time he needed to privately grieve and I had to respect that. "Where is Madison?"

"Suzanna still has her. I thought she would have been back by now, but I'm sure she'll bring her in a few minutes. We just ordered breakfast from the cafeteria; do you want anything?"

"No, I don't think I can eat right now."

"Are you okay?" I asked.

"Yeah, I'm fine. I had some coffee, but I just don't want anything to eat right now."

There was a knock at the door and Momma answered it for us. It was Suzanna. "I have your sweet girl with me. Are you ready to have her back now?"

"Of course we are," Momma said as she reached for the small basket.

"I am sorry; it took a little longer than expected. Cynthia and I wanted to take our time and do some special things with her. And you won't believe this, but she really surprised us."

"How so?" Chris inquired.

"Cynthia and I were taking a few pictures of her and we noticed that her heart was beating," Suzanna said.

In concert, the three of us responded with disbelief, "Her heart was beating?!"

"Yes, we couldn't believe it either. She just wasn't ready to go yet. We stopped taking pictures and sang, "Jesus Loves Me," to her until she went to be with Jesus. I just wanted ya'll to know that she did not go alone. We held her, loved on her, and released her to be at peace and it was such a beautiful experience," Suzanna said as her face beamed with pride.

"Wow, thank you. Thank you so much," Chris said. All I could do was smile and cry at the beauty of her passing. We were comforted to know that Madison was ushered into eternity with love, just like Grandma was.

Cynthia entered our room with a purple shopping bag filled with a matching memory box. She had also put a lavender sign with butterflies on the door stating, "No visitors please." The sign was also a way to communicate to the staff that we were a grieving family who had just experienced a loss. The memory box contained a tiny beaded bracelet with Madison's name, a silver butterfly charm, a white handkerchief, the measuring tape that was used to measure her body, pamphlets on grief and so much more. The most special memory in the box was a small white photo album containing the pictures that she and Suzanna captured of Madison. One of the staff members had processed the pictures at a one hour photo lab and rushed back to the hospital so that we could have the pictures right away.

Krista, the sonographer from Dr. Halton's office, came to visit during her lunch hour. She had become one of our biggest cheerleaders and supporters since our pregnancy with Briauna. She knew all of our history with attempts to build a family and had become part of our family as well. "We got the call from Dr. Laurel a few hours ago. All of the ladies at the office are hurting so badly for you both. I just wanted to come over to cry with you," she said with a tremble in her voice.

She wrapped her strong, petite arms around me and we cried together. She hugged Chris as she wiped tears from her face. "Dr. Halton will be around to see you this afternoon when he makes rounds. I'm sure he wants to give y'all a hug too." Her visit was brief, but comforting beyond words.

I was so impressed with the level of compassion and detail involved in every aspect of our care. We could clearly see that the staff from the hospital and the physician's offices consistently exceeded our expectations to care for our medical needs. Although our hearts were broken, the display of genuine love and concern served as a balm to soothe us.

The day came to a close and we were exhausted. Thankfully, we did not have many visitors and were able to spend all day with Madison without feeling like we needed to put her away when company arrived. Before reclining for the night, we decided to send Madison to the morgue for a few hours so that Chris and I could get a few hours of sleep.

Somehow, I managed to sleep peacefully the entire night, but woke up before dawn feeling like a horrible mother. I immediately pressed the call light, "Please have my nurse bring my baby back."

My heart raced as I waited for the door to swing open. Before the first knock on the door was complete, I yelled, "Come in!"

Madison was brought into the room in a clear bassinet, just like all of the other babies are transported. There was one noticeable difference however. The bassinet was covered with two hospital blankets. Perhaps it was the standard procedure when transporting deceased babies. I was not bothered by the fact that she was covered. I'm certain that the procedure was intended to respect the dignity of the deceased and not to cause alarm to others. "Here she is. I wrapped her in a warm blanket for you."

I didn't hear anything else the nurse said to me. I received Madison from her and immediately put her on my chest. I could immediately feel her ice cold face against my warm body. Guilt and remorse greeted me as I thought of my selfishness. How could I have been so careless? I missed my one opportunity to hold her through the night. I had the rest of my life to catch up on sleep. While I slept in a comfortable bed, she was locked in a dark freezer alone on a shelf.

The mental picture that I had envisioned caused my heart to sink to my toes. I held her tightly and apologized for sending her to the morgue. I spent every moment making up for lost time. I surveyed every inch of her body and tried to tuck away the visual memory of every detail. There was a faint knock at the door. "Come in."

The door slowly opened and Dr. Halton walked in. He was making his early morning rounds prior to starting his day at the office. He did not utter a word as he entered, he just hugged me tightly. "I'm so very sorry. No one deserves to have children more than you two," he said compassionately.

"Thank you."

Chris was asleep in the recliner so his voice never climbed above a whisper. "I wanted to come in to see you guys yesterday. Well, actually I did, but could not bring myself to come into the room. This is hard for me and I can only imagine how hard it is for the two of you."

"I understand. It's okay."

"She is beautiful. I didn't know you still had her here with you."

"I sent her to the morgue last night. I'm just trying to spend as much time as I can with her before we go home today."

Dr. Halton sat at the end of my hospital bed and confirmed that we did everything right. He encouraged us not to give up on our dream of building a family. He wanted us to have children just as much as we wanted them for ourselves. Dr. Halton was willing to do anything in his power to ensure that we never knew the pain of loss again. Prior to leaving, he reassured me that we would be in his prayers and we could call him if we needed to talk about anything.

After several early morning calls from our friends and family, my heart began to race. I knew Dr. Laurel would be making his rounds by early noon. I knew the routine all too well and anticipated him writing discharge orders with a plan to follow up in six weeks. Quickly, I retraced all of our actions with Madison and made sure that we told her everything we needed to say. I reviewed my digital camera to make sure that there were pictures of her with her dad, her grandma, and I. There were pictures of everything I wanted, but it still didn't seem like enough to maximize her memory for a lifetime.

Suzanna came into the room and I was so relieved that she was our nurse. She just had an extraordinary knack for caring for grieving families. "Good morning to you precious girl," she said with her southern dialect and an infectious smile.

"Good morning. How are you?" I said returning the same smile.

"I'm fine. Were you and Chris able to get any rest last night?"

"Actually, we both slept. Chris, as you can see is really enjoying his sleep. He was exhausted mentally and physically. I slept until four o'clock and called for the nurse to bring Miss Madison back in here. I figured that we'd likely go home today and I..." paused to wipe the tears that suddenly appeared.

"I understand completely. You wanted to spend as much time with your precious girl as you could before you leave this place today." Her right hand was on my shoulder and she was holding the box of Kleenex with the other hand. I assumed that she remembered how difficult it was for us to leave the hospital with Briauna.

Suzanna was the bereavement nurse for the hospital. She had seen her share of heavy hearts and empty arms leave the hospital and knew how valuable each moment was. "How do you always know exactly what to say, Suzanna?"

"I don't always feel like I know what to say. But I always remember how I felt when I lost my children."

"You have lost children too?" I asked in amazement.

"Oh yeah, I have two precious ones watching over me and our family in heaven. My losses happened almost eighteen years ago. I cannot forget them; they are still a part of me."

"Oh Suzanna, I had no idea. I'm sorry that it happened to you. Did you have boys or girls?"

"I'm not sure because my losses were very early miscarriages. I did not get the chance to see them on ultrasounds, know their gender or even pick out a name. I often wonder who and what they would have become. I am a nurse today because of them. I wanted to find a career where I could constantly be reminded of their lives. I also wanted a way to sincerely help other families who walk through the valley of death. This job allows me to do what I love, while honoring my children."

At last, I knew without question why Suzanna was so understanding and effective in her job. She was me and so many other childless mothers. Clearly, she had turned her pain into passion. Hearing her story made my appreciation for her personally and professionally grow exponentially. "Take all the time you need. We are not in a rush at all. If you are not ready to leave the hospital, we can let Dr. Laurel know that too. We'll do whatever you and Chris wants to do."

Chris and I talked about our feelings. He was extremely sad and I could see that he was in the throes of his grief. He was quiet, withdrawn, and emotionally fragile. I was deeply saddened, but it was coupled with pride. I was so proud that Madison defied the odds. I was proud that she skewed the statistics for the life-span of a nineteen week old baby. I was proud to actually feel like a mother for the first time and hold a living baby, rather than just carry one in my womb. "Should we go home today or should we stay?" I asked as I clutched Madison close to me. I was fearful of an emphatic "yes, we should leave."

His soft answer of, "It's up to you Babe. We can stay until you're ready to go."

He put the pressure of goodbye on me. I did not want to make the decision at all. "But Chris, what do you want to do? Your emotions and feelings are equally as important as mine."

After a long pause he said, "I'm okay if we leave or stay. We should just let Dr. Laurel decide what's best depending on how you are physically recovering." His suggestion worked for me. Neither of us had to decide when to leave our daughter. In the recesses of my mind, however, I knew from our past experiences that Dr. Laurel would release us. We were not ready for life after the discharge.

Suzanna came in the room to take my vitals and remove my IV. She informed me that Dr. Laurel would be on the floor by one o'clock. He said we could go home as long as my blood counts did not show any signs of infection.

"Do you want me to start gathering your discharge paperwork?" Suzanna asked.

"Yes, that'll be fine."

"I'll get everything together, but if you change your mind or want to hold off for a few hours we can do that also. There is no pressure to leave and there is certainly no rush."

Suzanna left the room and my heart nearly beat out of my chest. I grabbed Madison from the tiny wicker basket and walked around the hospital room with her. I went through my mental checklist again to make sure she would be well prepared for her journey into eternity. Closing my eyes, I savored how her small fragile body felt in my arms. If only I could have bottled up that moment, I would revisit it daily.

"Do you want to hold her for a while, Babe?"

"Yeah, I'll take her," he replied in a soft, excited whisper. Chris was exceptionally cautious in how he handled her and seemingly glided across the floor back to his seat. He held her hand and gazed intently at her face, which bore a striking resemblance to his. There were no audible words, but I'm sure his mind was inundated with thoughts and expressions of love that were too difficult to convey.

I sat in my hospital bed and watched Chris and Madison together. Despite the cloud of sadness that hovered over our room, I saw glimpses of sunshine. Perhaps the sunshine was the brief smile that framed Chris's face as he stroked her face with his finger or the delicate kiss he placed on her forehead. I wondered if he was thinking of starting tomorrow without her or imagining what the many tomorrows would have been like with her. No matter what his thoughts were, I was mesmerized by their father-daughter relationship and his gentleness with her.

"I think I should start packing our things. It's almost time for Dr. Laurel to make his rounds," he said in a quiet voice.

I did not realize that it was so late. *'Where did the morning go?'* I thought. "I want to take a shower and get dressed. Would you mind if we called Suzanna to come and get Madison while I'm in the shower? I just don't want to say goodbye again or have the visual image of leaving her behind," I said gathering the Kleenex to wipe my face before a tear made it to my chin. By that time I was in Chris's arms.

I buried my face into his neck and we both released the reservoir of tears we had bottled up. I could feel our hearts beating at the same fast tempo as we held each other tightly. The reality of our desire to build a family was despondently painful. Clearly, we were on the wrong side of the statistics and zero for three on the scoreboard. "This isn't fair, Babe. Why does everyone else get to have a family except us?"

"I wish I had the answer. I've been asking myself the same question," he said.

No matter how much pain we had at the moment, I knew we would both find the courage to dream again. Death was no match for the deep yearning in our hearts for children. "I'm going to get in the shower."

As I slowly walked passed Madison and was drawn to her. I gave her five kisses: one for each of her sisters and my two beloved grandmas and one for her. Then I walked into the shower without looking back. I hurriedly turned the shower on and began to sing every hymn I knew, so that I wouldn't hear Chris make the call to Suzanna. More importantly, I did not want to know the moment when she officially left our room. I simply wanted to send her off with singing rather than silence and sadness.

I stayed in the shower until the water turned cold. I cautiously exited my safe haven and listened for voices, but I only heard the TV. I peeped from the bathroom and asked, "Are you okay?"

"Yes, I'm fine. Suzanna got Madison a while ago. Cynthia also stopped by to check on us and left these papers to complete her birth certificate. She's visiting another patient, but she'll be back around shortly. We need to decide on either having a service, cremation, or private burial," he advised.

Somehow, I had not considered all of the decisions that we'd have to make. I didn't want to think about anything. And I most assuredly did not want a multitude of family, friends, or even strangers approaching us at a service to say, "It was for the best." or any other asinine cliché that could possibly comfort us. "I don't know how you feel, but I'd rather have her cremated. At least we would have her at home with us. What do you want to do, Babe?"

"I do not want a service; cremation is fine in my opinion," he said matter-of-factly.

"Cremation it is. Now, let's complete the birth certificate." This was the first time that we ever had to complete the form. I had to stop writing my social security number and be thankful for the new experience of holding a living, breathing baby.

Cynthia returned to our room with a large purple shopping bag just as I completed the form. We were all too familiar with the purple bag. It's the official consolation prize given to families who do not get to leave the hospital with their children. Although I loathed the reason for being the recipient of this award, it was filled with priceless treasures of Madison's life. Nearly everything that touched her body was in the bag.

The keepsakes included: the measuring tape used to measure her length, the purple blanket she was wrapped in, every outfit that she was photographed in, the small artificial rose that was placed beside her for pictures, a small beaded name bracelet and a lavender and pearl bracelet for me . There were also poems specifically for the grieving mother and one for the grieving dad. The greatest surprise was a clay tin with an imprint of Madison's tiny feet, which were no bigger than the pad of my index finger. A smiled formed on my face through the tears as I recounted feeling her forceful kicks during the night.

BUILDING A FAMILY BREAKS MY HEART

With discharge paperwork in hand, we were ready to leave the hospital. Chris left to move the car to the entrance. I refused a wheel chair and opted to walk out of the building with Cynthia's assistance. This was my attempt to look as normal as possible to any passersby. My head was lifted and my eyes were intensely focused on each room number affixed to the wall. Passing room 443 was a breeze. Passing room 441 was effortless until I took one step toward room 439. My heart sank into my empty womb as I gazed into the empty room and remembered our first encounter with death and Destiny. "Are you okay? Should I get a wheelchair?" Cynthia asked.

"No, it's okay. I just needed to stop right here." My hand touched the Braille number plate on the wall as I sighed inwardly. Thoughts from December 19, 2007 replayed in my mind like a movie. My feet were fastened to the floor and my eyes were glued to the empty bed. Perhaps if I stayed there long enough, the faded vision of Destiny would become clear again.

"Tanika, are you sure you don't need a wheelchair?"

"Oh! No, I'm fine. I'm ready now."

Thankfully, no one passed us in the hallway or in the lobby. Chris was waiting outside the car as we exited the building. He saw the glassy look in my eyes, put his strong hands around my waist and whispered softly in my ear, "It's okay, Babe. We will be back one day." I nodded my head in agreement and eased into my seat. Cynthia hugged both of us and said goodbye.

Chapter 13
Silent Communication

We drove in silence to Halley's Mortuary. Thankfully, Cynthia had already called the owner and provided most of our information. The staff was expecting us and graciously welcomed our arrival. We were escorted to a beautifully decorated, dimly lit show room. Coffins of different colors and sizes were mounted on the walls. There were beautiful instrumental hymns being played over the sound system.

The stillness and peace of the mortuary were indescribable. "Mr. & Mrs. Dillard, I'm the owner, Tom. Let me first say how deeply sorry I am that you all lost your daughter, Madison. I know you just left the hospital, so I promise to be brief. There are just a few things I need from you and then I'll be happy to answer any questions you may have. Is that okay?"

"Yes, that will be fine. Thank you," Chris answered.

We both had to provide our driver's licenses and sign the consent for cremation. Tom explained the process and advised that Madison's creamains would be available for pick up in approximately ten days. "If you have a stuffed animal or blanket that you would like her to have, feel free to drop it by in the next few days. We will ensure that your keepsakes accompany Madison to the crematory."

Tom gave us a black folder embossed with grey wording and design with all of our paperwork. He also included a copy of his business card. He urged us to call him if we had any questions or if we decided to provide a keepsake for Madison.

We drove home in silence with a box of tissues in my lap that we both shared. There were simply no words in the English language to describe the heaviness in our fragile hearts. I rubbed Chris's hand or leg for the entire twenty-five minute drive home. I wanted to convey the message of, "I'm here for you. I love you, and I'm so sorry that this has happened to us again." I just could not get the boulder-sized lump out of my throat to say anything. Rubbing his warm skin was the best comfort that I could offer.

We walked into our cold home and the silence magnified in my soul. Our house was nothing like I had hoped it to be. Nowhere even close. There were no pink balloons to display on the mailbox. There was no need for a stork in the front yard to proclaim the arrival of our little princess. The black cloud that covered our house was enough.

Chris unpacked the car and put the memory bag in the planned nursery, which was still a guestroom. I opted to rest for the remainder of the afternoon and encouraged Chris to do the same. We were both in bed quietly watching the ceiling fan. We tried to rest, but our minds were at the hospital and mortuary. "I wonder if Madison is there yet." Chris asked.

"I don't know, but I can call Tom and find out."

I reached for my cell phone and saw that I had two missed calls. One was from Momma and the other from the mortuary. I listened to the message and it was Lisa, the receptionist, calling to inform us that Madison arrived to the mortuary shortly after three o'clock. Finally, we were able to rest knowing that Madison was safe. We turned our cell phones off and closed our eyes in our all too familiar, painfully quiet home.

We woke up when the doorbell rang at a quarter till seven that evening. "Hey Momma, come on in," Chris said as he rose from his slumber.

"I have been so worried. I kept calling, but I couldn't get either of you to pick up. Are y'all okay?"

"Yes ma'am, we're fine. We were exhausted when we came in, so we went directly to bed. Tanika is in the bedroom; you can go see her."

"Knock, Knock!"

"Hey Ma," I replied softly.

Momma sat on the edge of the bed and wrapped her arms tightly around me. "How are you feeling?"

I rested my cheek on her shoulder and my tears fell on her gray silk blouse. Words failed me. I could not describe how I felt. Physically, I felt fairly fine with the exception of some cramping. Emotionally, I was distressed, perplexed, grateful, sad, proud, mad, and a multitude of other contrasting feelings. "It's okay. It's okay! I don't know exactly what you are feeling. But I do know how much it hurts me to see you and Chris go through this again. It's hard for me to even imagine the pain. Y'all are going to get through this. I promise you will. We've just got to keep on trusting and believing that God will hear our prayers."

"Yes ma'am," I said in a tired voice.

I tried to go back to sleep, but I couldn't. There were so many thoughts in my head and on my heart. I pulled out the laptop and began writing a blog update. Lately, I had been pretty lousy with posting regular activity. However, this was one easy way to inform everyone of how we were doing rather than duplicating the response several times a day. Besides, neither one of us wanted to communicate with anyone other than each other.

Chapter 14
The Blogs

My blog became my sanctuary. I felt safe emptying my heart and the thoughts in my head onto the keyboard. Hiding behind the screen was the most fitting place for me.

Blog entry: July 31, 2009

If anyone would have ever written a story of my life they would never have imagined that we would be remotely talking about having a third miscarriage. Unfortunately, the words you are reading are painfully true. Our sweet Madison Noelle was born on Thursday morning, July 31st at 3:10 am. Our tiny miracle's cord was tightly wrapped around her neck, but she lived until 10:50 am.

The doctors and nurses were astonished because the lungs of a nineteen week old baby are not compatible with life by their knowledge, thus no heroic measures could be done to save her. The medical staff just stood by quietly waiting for her to take her last breath. After nearly thirty minutes they left in amazement. Indeed, Madison was a fighter! When her breathing got a little shallow I would breathe on her and gently whisper, "Live Madison," and she quickly responded.

Madison was held and loved every minute of her life. We made sure to tell her of our love for her, sing to her and simply ask her to kiss her sisters, Destiny and Briauna for us. If any of you know my Momma, you know that her grand kids are her greatest joy. So, Madison had a whopping dose of the infamous "baby talk," that only she can do.

In a previous post I stated that Madison would look like me and act like my husband Chris. I was completely wrong. She was her Daddy's twin. The only things she had from me were long legs, feet, and fingers. She even had the line in Chris' forehead, his round head and the dimple in his chin. I just carried her, but what an honor to carry such tenacious life from an incredible seed of an awesome man.

Our bittersweet hello/goodbye touched Chris and I to the very core of our being. Everything we thought we knew about God has been challenged and we still have so many questions that are unanswered. The more we seek for answers the more frustrated we become. We've heard ALL (and I do mean every last one) of the religious clichés and cannot take another. We have also heard ALL of the sympathy imaginable with the losses of Destiny and Briauna...can't take any more of that either.

*One thing I am sure of is a clause in John 16:33... **"In the world you have trouble."** Can I just insert THREE check marks beside that clause, please??? The remainder of the Scripture says, "but have **confidence (or be of good cheer.) I have overcome the world."***

Confidence and cheer are not what we feel at the moment. Please understand clearly...WE ARE NOT LEAVING GOD (we have nowhere else to go.) We are having a HUMAN EXPERIENCE and it's tough. Trying to wrap our minds around the reason for three perfect little girls to be given to us and snatched away from our reach because of my flawed body is simply unfathomable and seemingly unfair.

The sad reality of leaving the hospital today with yet another memory box and no baby was more than we wanted to handle. Our first trip after leaving the hospital was to the mortuary to make arrangements for Madison's cremation. That just doesn't seem right! We should have been hurrying home with her in December to get her ready for her 1st Christmas.

Despite the outcome, we have to thank all of you who have labored in prayer for us, made yourself available to us, encouraged us, and shared this human experience with us in any other action. We are thankful for you. We don't know what to say and we don't want you to feel like you have to say anything more to comfort us. Although we have chosen not to receive company or take phone calls right now, know that we indeed feel the love and prayers for us and we are deeply touched and moved to tears by your heartfelt compassion.

Blog entry: August 5, 2009
"If only in my dreams!"

  I have sat at the computer nearly every day reading blog comments and then attempting to post a new blog. Seemingly, the words would just not come together – not really sure that today will be any different.
  Let me first start by saying a big thank you. We have been blessed with great friends, family, and coworkers to love and support us. Although we have closed ourselves off to many calls and visits we are very much aware of your thoughts and concern for us, thank you!
  I have to be honest and say that we do not understand why losses continue to befall us. There is nothing more that we want than to be parents and to love a child as much as we love each other, which is a whole lot. Chris seems to think that God really trusts us and that He has great plans for us. This may very well be true, but I didn't know that the trust and favor of God could cause so much pain. I really had to think of a reason to live. There have been days when I just want to be with my girls. Despite my indescribable longing for them, I have to get up and live for the day that we hold and bring home the manifestation of our prayers. Until that time, we are determined to live through this!
  There will be a day that this all makes sense. I really don't understand God, but we are going to have to trust Him with everything. I need to find the same trust that I sang about at Grandma's house when I was a kid. I think I will sing that hymn on my heart today and in the days to come and see what happens.
  I will bring my rambling to an end with this last thought; Have you ever had such an amazing dream that you didn't want to be awakened from? I'm sure we all have. Sunday night, I had the best dream! Chris and I had our sweet Madison at home and we were feeding her and being proud parents. How I wish that dream was a reality. Madison, we'll hold you close to us in our hearts AND in our dreams!

Blog entry: August 10, 2009
"*Scattered thoughts...*"

Thought 1:

Chris and I left for Myrtle Beach on Wednesday and came back on Saturday. It was so nice to get out from under the seeming veil of depression here at home. We had a good trip, but there were still painful reminders of why we were really there. Every time I saw a pregnant woman I couldn't hold back the tears. Specifically, on our 1st day at the beach, a pregnant lady walked past and stopped right in front of us and held her stomach. It appeared that she was contracting. I wanted to run to her and help her because her husband was walking fifteen steps ahead of her and didn't come back to help. There was nothing I could do.
    Secondly, there were plenty of strollers and infants in the arms of their parents. It was a beautiful sight, but just made me sad. The good part about all of this is, absolutely no one knew us or our story. It's just hard to face people right now. If we could relocate and have a home, our jobs, our family and our church I would be packing today. I know it's not reality, but certainly what I'd do if I could.
    I feel like the woman with the issue of blood. Although, our "issues" are different, we share some of the same feelings of shame and isolation. This woman wanted nothing more than to touch Jesus and be made whole. I simply need Jesus to touch ME and make me whole – spiritually, mentally, physically, and emotionally!

Thought 2:

I have a few things on the to-do list for this week:
- Complete and mail birth and death certificate forms;
- Pick up Madison's cremains from the mortuary;
- Have Madison's name and birth date engraved on her urn;

- *Order pictures that we took of Madison to complete her memory book;*
- *Schedule my two week follow up appointment with my OB;*
- *Talk with my high risk OB about abdominal cerclage surgery and timing for placement;*
- *Find an expert to place my cerclage;*
- *Look for grief counselors in the area. I went to a counselor in October, but I wouldn't recommend her again. She got on my nerves and would have me do these weekly assignments, but when I would go back the next week she had no idea what she assigned me to do. UGH...I really don't want to see a Christian counselor. The last thing I want is for someone to try to explain God to me and why this is happening to us. No one knows and it's just too frustrating to even discuss.*
- *Buy some kind of decongestant to dry up my milk supply. This is just too painful (both mental and physical) that there is no baby to feed!*

__Thought 3:__

Chris's bereavement leave is over and he went back to work today. We went out to dinner yesterday and I started crying just thinking about him returning. While I ironed his uniform I cried. He is the best medicine for me and I feel so incredibly blessed to have such an awesome husband. I also have to think about going back to work. It scares me to think about just concentrating on a project for work, my attitude, and how I will be able to interact with others. SCARY!!!

Enough rambling for today...

Blog entry: August 18, 2009
"Picking up the pieces..."

  I was able to tackle some of my "to-do" list from last week. Specifically, the most important thing that I wanted to do was to pick up Madison's cremains from the mortuary. I prepared myself to have a break down right in the parking lot of the mortuary. Surprisingly, none of the anticipated emotional responses happened at all. I looked at the bag of ashes containing tiny bone fragments and experienced a rush of various feelings. I was amazed that she had been reduced to dust. I was clammy and weak, but I felt proud to just hold "her" again. It was sad because I wasn't carrying her inside of me, but rather beside me in the passenger seat. Our heart has seemingly shattered, however, I felt like I picked up some of the pieces.
  I still had some medical things to take care of and my two-week follow up appointment on Thursday. I go to a single practice OB; therefore, the office is small and only has two exam rooms. It goes without saying that going back to the office is bittersweet. There are so many happy memories there and a few sad ones that seem to overshadow the happy ones.
  They said that I have upper and lower cervical scarring from the vaginal cerclage. I can understand the lower scarring since that is where the cerclage was placed, but I don't know how the upper scarring occurred. At any rate, there is nothing that can be done about it and I don't think it will cause any issue with future pregnancies.
  My most exciting find was a wonderful gynecologic surgeon in Chicago. Maya, one of my blog followers from California, commented on my last blog. She encouraged me to research Dr. Harper McDonald. He is affectionately referred to as Dr. H., and is known around the world for his work with Transabdominal cerclages (TAC). He performs over 100 per year and has a 95% success rate in full term delivery.
  Women with cervical issues have traveled from as far away as Australia to have Dr. H. perform their TAC. I

emailed him and gave him a brief description of my story and wanted to get more information. Within four hours he had e-mailed me back with a long, detailed reply. He was a very nice guy and amazingly, he knew my high-risk OB here. He and Dr. Halton were undergrad students together. I felt like I was connecting the dots! Dr. H. says the TAC is most effective when placed pre-pregnancy. The earliest it can be placed is September 24th – exactly eight weeks post Madison's birth.

I have a phone consult with Dr. H. on Friday and we will finalize the date of the surgery. I'm headed to Chicago! The other good thing from Dr. H. is that we can try again as soon as the TAC is placed. We will soon be on our way to building a family that we can bring home.

I received full maternity leave through September ninth, but I decided to go back on August 24th. Am I ready? Absolutely NOT! Do I need to? ABSOLUTELY YES! Chris and I had several discussions about when to go back to work. He simply wanted me to take my time and go back only when I was ready. It's NOW or NEVER for me.

Home has been my place of safety. I sat in the house most of last week with doors closed, curtains drawn, TV off and drowning in my own thoughts and tears. Getting out of bed and taking a shower was a major accomplishment. It would take me all morning and afternoon to decide what to cook for dinner. But somehow, I would be totally fine with things remaining just the way they are. I have to go back to work now or else become a permanent fixture at home.

My plan this week is to go somewhere every day, just to get out of the house. I have to deal with the shame and embarrassment, and even the silence that comes with my presence. So yesterday my excursions were the office, the mall, and the grocery store. Today, I am going to my support group meeting; not as the group leader, but as a grieving mother who is determined to survive.

Blog Entry: August 21, 2009
"I love Dr. H!!!"

  My phone consult went great today! Dr. H. is very thorough. The list of questions we had were answered during his overview. Although he has copies of my medical records, he wanted to hear about our losses. I started, "My first miscarriage..."
  He immediately stopped me and said, "Mrs. Dillard, we typically classify miscarriage as a first trimester loss, which usually happens because of genetic abnormalities or unknown reasons. What you have experienced should not be minimized as just a miscarriage. You've had three second trimester losses. You and your husband held three babies."
  So, I preceded with the story of our three second trimester losses. Dr. H. asked the standard medical history. I confirmed that I had no medical issues. His next statement made me smile, "Mrs. Dillard, I need for you and Chris to start thinking and believing that you can have ALL of the children you want and that you will have normal full-term pregnancies." Oh, the joy that filled my soul upon hearing these words.
  Dr. H. proceeded to explain the malfunctioning of my cervix, as I have never heard it explained before. He narrated how things should happen in a normal cervix. Finally, he explained the surgical process. There will be a band placed at the top of the cervix to prevent it from opening. He explained that this method is basically 100% effective, because there is no way the cervix can open bigger than the band around it.
  The scheduler was out of the office until Monday. I should receive follow up communication then with the confirmed surgery date. Let the countdown begin! I will not be able to drive for 7-10 days post-op, but should be able to do other activities in no time.
  Dr. H. ended the conversation by restating his initial statement, "I need for you and your husband to start thinking and believing that you can have ALL of the children you want

and that you will have normal, full-term pregnancies. However, there is just one thing that your husband has to do for me."

"I am certain that he is willing to do everything in his power to ensure that we have children we can bring home alive and healthy. So, just let us know what he needs to do."

Dr. H. paused, then chuckled loudly, "He just has to get you pregnant, Mrs. Dillard. Everything else will be fine."

"Dr. H, don't worry, he'll be more than happy to. We'll see you in September!!!"

Blog Entry: August 23, 2009
"Jesus travels through the mail!!!"

I am so incredibly touched. Last week a card came in the mail from someone I've never met. Although we do not know each other personally, our husbands work together. This sweet lady and her circle of friends knew about our story and had been praying for us even before we conceived Madison. She sent me the sweetest card that simply encouraged my faith and reminded me that God will guide us through this time.

I stood at my front door and cried a river just knowing how much God thinks about us and our situation. How touching it is to know that people give unselfishly of their time and of themselves to pray earnestly for strangers. Many of you reading this have simply heard of our story and have prayed for us. Please know that we sincerely feel the effects of your prayers and are indeed humbled and appreciative.

On Saturday, we received another card from three couples we attend church with. Again, I could not hold back the tears. We had a very elegant, homemade card filled with artistic craftsmanship and love. This card touched us tremendously. We have received NUMEROUS cards in the mail over the last month and we've read them all and placed them in Madison's memory box. This card however, was very unique. It was not a sympathy card, but rather a card to inspire us to keep doing what we love to do and that is to love each other. Through the tears I was able to smile and reflect on the love that Chris and I share. The love we have for our family and friends, and the love that God shows to us; even through the mail.

Can I challenge you? Can you take forty-four cents and brighten someone's day or send it in an e-mail? Just send a card to an old friend, a relative, or perhaps a stranger. Just tell them that you love them, appreciate them, or whatever it may be to give them hope.

I sent out several cards over the weekend and I can honestly say that it feels equally overwhelming to give love as to receive it. Our precious spiritual godfather, "Pop Dawkins" says, "Love is what it DOES." If you love someone, don't just say it; do something to show it! Love makes the journey of life worth living.

Now, back to work!!!

The day has finally arrived! I am facing my fears of getting back to work. I had some thoughts today like, 'WHAT was I thinking? Am I really ready?' and so forth. Well, none of that matters because I will be at work tomorrow and there's no turning back now. I will make it a good day. I am thankful that I never have to do anything alone or in my own strength. "God, thank you for going before me and enabling me to face the challenges of tomorrow."

Blog entry: September 1, 2009
"Don't waste pain"

Today has been a great day and my mind has been in overdrive. My friend Summer said, "I'm so impressed with your perseverant spirit! Please tell me how you do it?"

This really caused me to think and reflect on the highs and lows of my life. I really thought, 'How have we <u>endured</u> this? Why do we manage to keep at it? Why not give up?'

A great theologian once said, **"Don't waste pain!"**

Okay, so this is what my husband said during his sermon last year. Allow me to call him a great theologian if I want to. But really, we made the decision not to waste the pain we've been through. It would be so incredibly easy to let our past pain define our lives. However, I don't want to be known for what we have lost. Do you know people like that? You always hear the negative and the gossip about people. "That's Sally, the one that got divorced. That's John's daughter, the one that's the drug addict," or "That's Tanika and Chris, the ones who lost three babies."

So, why have I persevered? Because, I am so much more than the pain I have endured. Pain has a purpose. It's just the method of transportation to get me to the next phase in my life. My pain cannot be the final verdict and description of me. I'm going to fully develop the pain. It's like developing a picture in a dark room where there is an absence of light.

Think about it. What if you never saw the finished product of your wedding photos? What if they were stopped in "process" and you only saw the black, wet paper. That is the only memory you'd have of your wedding to pass along for generations. This is exactly how I could be if I let my pain define me. I could stay here and become emotionally bitter and negative, but I'm not accustomed to darkness! I have to know this is just a snapshot in time and not the end. This is process! When pain is fully developed, something of value comes from it. So stay tuned. Don't define me by my moment of darkness. Just keep watching for the final picture. "Arise; shine for thy light has come!"

Blog entry: September 7, 2009
"Conflicting times"

Have you ever felt like everything is great and awful at the same time? Today is really one of those days with no extreme highs and no frigid lows, just questionable mediums.

My mind has been in overdrive today and I can't quite seem to downshift. My thoughts have not been about our daughters, but mostly about life and people in it.

This weekend has been exceptionally wonderful for me. I spent time with people I love the most--my family! Man, we had such fun! I felt such peace being in a room with generations of wise people who I knew genuinely loved each other, had no wrong motives, intentions, or ill will toward one another. We shared good food, meaningful embraces, and unforgettable laughter, but time passed all too fast. **It was the best of times.**

In the midst of the "highs," the "lows" invade my space like the dark, howling winds of a hurricane. I am compelled to process these thoughts in my head, unless I let them overtake me. I grieve the hollowness of meaningless chatter and actions laced with motives arrayed in the wardrobe of comradery. I grieve for words misspoken or never spoken at all. I applaud the few who seek the light of truth. I grieve for those who feel safe in the darkness of lies. **It was the worst of times.**

"Lord, You are an infinite God without end or beginning. Not only are You aware of all I have ever been or experienced, You are aware of all there is to come. In fact, You have already been there and know me – know all I have experienced from moment to moment. You have experienced my life in an intimate way even to the numbering of the hairs on my head. Every detail of my life is important and valuable to You.

Though I am constrained in my thinking as it relates to time, You are not. The greatest hindrance to not living a life outside the constraints of time is to see it limited and unyielding, to see time as having no potential outside of the moment. To do so eliminates all consequences and blessings resulting out of time-based actions on my part. Time is eternal and I must see it as such. What I do in time affects the times to come; therefore, it has eternal consequences both good and bad."

"Teach me to see beyond the moment into a realm where there is no time so I can put more value on what I do at any given time. Teach me to see everything I do with eternal eyes. As I do this, what I participate in or don't participate in will change in order to bring about the most effective change."

Blog entry: September 13, 2009
"I believe..."

There are angels among us! I came home yesterday afternoon to find a package on my front door step. My first thought was that my husband was doing some more cyber shopping. To my surprise, the package was for me! So I started to think, 'Did I order something? Did I sign up for something?'

The package was from a Christian ministry offering help, encouragement, and hope for women experiencing infertility or loss of a baby due to miscarriage, stillbirth, and early infant loss. So, I ripped it open to find out who sent this gift to me. The package contained, "Learning through Loss," a self-guided Bible study designed to encourage the women who are grieving and an audio CD of a mother sharing her testimony of God's faithfulness to her. There was no information about who sent it!

This is such a thoughtful gift, but even more than that, I was amazed at the timing of it all. Yesterday was an emotional day for me. I spent some time doing retail therapy, but everywhere I went, I saw pregnant women and babies. I even found myself browsing through the kids section of a department store with smiles and tears. While driving home, I had a good cry and an awakening moment which revealed why I was so emotional. It was this time two years ago that our life was normal and untouched by loss. It was two years ago that I had my first positive pregnancy test. We were blissfully happy! My tears were my way of reflecting on the yesterdays and longing for happier tomorrows.

I was reminded of God's faithfulness toward me. I was reminded that nothing takes God by surprise and no matter what I will ever face, I am never alone. I believe God places people in our lives for His purpose. I am thankful and humbled by the orchestration and strategic nature of God.

I am so sure this gift is going to be a blessing to so many people. I intend to share the information every occasion that I can. I co-lead a grief and loss support group in our area and I am sure we will be able to utilize this to help other grieving parents. I believe – There are angels among us!

Blog entry: September 20, 2009
"Untitled"

Can you believe that by this time next week I will be back at home with my abdominal cerclage? I am so happy and nervous at the same time. It seems like I have a million things to do before flying out on Wednesday. They will all get done even if it doesn't happen until the wee hours of the morning. I packed my clothes tonight and need to pack the toiletries on Tuesday.

I have made my list of the things that I cannot forget: phone charger, music, pain medicine and one of Chris's t-shirts. I need to have something with his scent close to me. It is a well known fact that I do not like being without my man. Momma is traveling with me. Chris has taken a large amount of his vacation time during my previous hospitalizations and bed rest. He will stay here to work, but will be in constant communication with Momma throughout the surgery.

This weekend was great rainy weather. I admit I did nothing but enjoy it! I spent the whole day inside yesterday, writing a speech for a memorial at our local hospital. I am not really sure how I consented to speak so soon after loss, but I am sure I will get through it just fine. The speech is actually coming along well. I do not feel compelled to just tell our story, but to offer hope to others as well. Recalling the journey of three losses was very emotional for me yesterday. I realized that I had suppressed a great deal of emotions. I also realized that God's strength really is perfect in weakness. I am just amazed that I lived through all of it.

The event is on the third Sunday in October. I will be sure to either post the speech after I give it or give an update about it. If you know of anyone who has been touched by miscarriage, stillbirth, or early infant loss, please encourage them to come to the event if you or they are in the area. You can e-mail me for details.

As much as I would love to continue this ramble, I can't! I still have a growing to-do list before me. We'll chat soon! Thank you all so much for your prayers and encouragement. Please continue to pray for traveling grace and pray for my surgeon that I already love so much, Dr. H.

Blog Entry: September 23, 2009
"The journey continues!"

On the road again – well, not exactly! In the air again is a more accurate statement. We've looked forward to this day and it's so close. My nervousness and excitement are parallel. I have thought about this so much that I started having psychosomatic rashes on my hands, arms, and legs. Leave it to me to make it interesting.

I am confident that the Lord has already gone before us. He has sent many wonderful people to cover us in prayer and be the voice of support and encouragement. I wanted God to heal me supernaturally so that His Glory would not have to be shared or channeled through the medical professionals. However, I'll gladly endure this. There is nothing more to lose. I believe in the wisdom of our God that ALL of this will be ultimately used to expand His reputation of faithfulness.

A few days before I delivered Destiny in Dec '07, I was dreaming of the song, "All For Your Glory." In my sleep, I was in the midst of an incredible praise & worship experience and this is the song ministered to me deeply. I woke up and penned the words to the song.

I KNOW that this is the message for the journey.

No matter what we gain, "It's for His Glory!"
No matter what we lose, "It's for His Glory!"
No matter who or what we encounter, "It's for His Glory!"

Thank you for your love and support. Big hugs and we'll chat soon!

For His Glory!
Tanika

Chapter 15
Rebuilding Me

While Chris drove me and my momma to the airport I had one hand tightly gripped on his leg while wiping tears with the other hand. I have never been graceful when it comes to departures. I simply do not like saying goodbye, even if just for a little while. "Will you just drop us off at the door? I don't want you to park and come inside of the airport."

"Why not? I was only planning to stay until you got settled," he said with a smile.

"That's the problem. As long as you are there, I'm going to cry."

"True, but you are going to do that whether I am with you or not."

"I know Babe, but it will likely be better for both of us if you drop us off at the door," I requested again. We arrived at the airport and said a prayer for safe travels and for the surgery. He quickly exited the car to gather our luggage from the trunk and embraced Momma. "Thank you so much for everything. I will call to check on y'all."

"Alright Son, I'll take good care of her."

"Dry your eyes, Babe. Before you know it, you'll be back at home," he said as he wrapped his strong arms around me, allowing me to have a good cry. "I love you. Now, stop crying and go get on the plane," he whispered, kissing my tear-stained face.

As Momma and I slowly walked through the automatic entrance doors of the airport I made one quick look over my shoulder and waved goodbye. Chris was wiping his eyes. Though he would likely never admit it, I am almost certain that our temporary parting caused him to shed a few tears. There was no need to let him know that I saw him crying. We continued our journey to the ticket counter and then the boarding gate. "Are you okay?" Momma asked quietly.

"Yes, ma'am. I am just a pathetic, emotional case when it comes to being without Chris. Even though I've traveled without him before, it doesn't get any easier."

We boarded the plane and settled in for the two hour and forty minute flight. I located my cell phone in my overstuffed purse and found that I had missed two calls from Chris and one from Lauren. "Please power down all electronic devices at this time and prepare for departure," the airline stewardess announced.

With no time to return their calls, I sent a text message to Chris. *"Babe, sorry I missed your calls. I'll call you when we land. Love you!"*

Before I could turn the phone off, his reply of, *"I love you more,"* flashed on my screen. With a smile on my face and a few skipped beats of my heart, I put my phone away.

The flight to Detroit was beautiful and serene. The sky was majestically painted blue and the clouds loomed like pillows from the heavens. With my face pressed against the small square window of the plane, I wondered if my girls could see me from above. My eyes were fixated on the canvas of earth beneath me. I had hopes of seeing a sign, perhaps a butterfly or a rainbow that would confirm an angelic presence accompanied us. Although I never saw a visual sign, I certainly felt the peace of a horde of angels, especially Destiny, Briauna, and Madison.

We caught the shuttle to our hotel and dropped our bags in the room. I called Chris as soon as we were settled and gave him our itinerary for the remainder of the evening. My momma and I migrated through the city like professional tourists and confirmed transportation to the hospital for the next day. We found a restaurant two blocks from the hotel called Blues and Bowties. It was the best seafood dinner, wine, and soulful music, making the perfect ending to our day.

There was so much adrenaline running through my veins that I could hardly sleep. I feared that my exhausted body would relish the coziness of the overstuffed down comforter and miss my 7:00 alarm. I tossed and turned, prayed about the surgery, drifted to sleep, woke up in a panic and watched the clock proceed toward daybreak.

Finally, 5:45 a.m. arrived. With the changing time zones, it was also time for Chris's work alarm to go off. I grabbed my phone. "Rise and shine, Babe."

"Good morning. What time is it?" he asked in a sluggish tone.

"It's time for you to be up. Your alarm should have gone off by now. It's a quarter 'til six."

"I was in a good sleep. The best that I've had in a while – I'm glad you called. How did you sleep?"

"Just okay. It was strange having the entire bed to myself. I did enjoy not being disturbed by your loud snoring. I can't believe that you slept so well without me," I laughed.

"So, how are you feeling about the surgery?"

"My mind has been going a hundred miles per minute for most of the night. I am a little nervous since this is my first invasive surgery and much different than the vaginal cerclage, but mostly excited. I'm ready to get this behind us and fill our home with a lot of kids. I hope you're ready."

"I know exactly what you mean, Babe. I'll keep you barefoot and pregnant for the next few years. That will not be a problem at all," he laughed out loud.

"Sounds like a good plan to me!"

"Everything will be perfect today. I have peace about it and there are so many people praying for us. The worst is over and it can only get better from here. You will be fine."

"Thanks Babe! I agree. Alright, I'll let you get ready for work. I'll leave a status update on your voicemail when we're at the hospital or I'll have Momma call you. Hopefully, I should be able to talk to you during your lunch break since the surgery is not until two o'clock. I still have another hour or more to sleep before my alarm goes off. I hope I can sleep as good as you did. I certainly need it, because it is going to be a long day."

"Alright, I'll let you go. Have a good day and I will talk to you soon. I love you."

"I love you too, Sir."

Taking full advantage of the queen-sized bed I stretched out like an eagle and closed my eyes. My body sank into the mattress and I fell fast asleep. It was the best sleep I had slept in the last twenty-four hours. The alarm clock sounded precisely at seven o'clock. Rather than hitting the snooze button, I disabled the alarm entirely. After all, I didn't have to be up so early.

Checkout was at eleven o'clock. Since I couldn't eat or drink anything there was no need to rush to breakfast. I only needed to repack the few essential toiletries that were removed from my luggage. My case was solid for returning to sleep without setting an additional alarm. Without delay, I returned to my comfortable sleep. There were no thoughts in my head and no dreams – just good sound slumber.

"Good Morning, Sunshine! Are you ready to get up now?"

"Morning Momma, what time is it?" I asked from under the covers.

"Just a few minutes after nine."

"Seriously?! I didn't expect to sleep that long, but it was just what I needed. How did you sleep?"

"Fairly well. I tell you, that bed was comfortable. If anybody was in the next room, I'm sure they heard your snoring. I'm surprised you didn't wake yourself up."

We both laughed as I unraveled the covers and sat up in bed. "Momma, you're already dressed?"

"Honey, yes. It is a beautiful day. I've already been downstairs for breakfast and walked a few blocks. "

"I didn't even hear you get up or leave. I suppose I need to start getting ready."

Moving at a steady snail's pace, I transformed from lethargic to energized with the aid of a hot shower. My anxiety was washed away and replaced with excitement and hope. Momma and I were dressed in our leisure suits ready to face the day.

The cab driver drove at the speed of light for the seven miles to Blythe General. We held on to our seatbelts tightly with hopes of a safe arrival. Thankfully, the driver was experienced and securely navigated us to the entrance doors of the massive hospital. We asked for directions and proceeded to the registration area to check in.

The process was exceptionally quick. I had already completed all of the required forms and medical history questionnaire electronically to make sure they had my medical records immediately after my surgery date was confirmed. I was determined not to let any grass grow under my feet. I signed two financial disclosures and was instructed to report to the nurse's desk on the seventh floor. "Hi, I'm Tanika. I have a surgery scheduled with Dr. McDonald today. This is my Mom, Katherine. She will be my caregiver."

"Well, good morning! I am Justine, the charge nurse for the unit. Welcome to Boston General," she said with an infectious smile.

"Thank you."

Grabbing a chart and pen, Justine advised us to follow her to room 714. "Come on in and have a seat. I have several questions to ask you before getting you prepared for surgery. Okay?"

"Alright, that's fine."

"Have you had anything to eat or drink since midnight?"

"No."

"Are you currently on any medications?"

"No."

"Do you have any drug allergies?"

"No."

"Date of your last menstrual period?"

"August 31st."

"How many pregnancies?"

"Three."

"How many living children?"

I paused briefly to recover from the unexpected question. "Three," I replied sharply followed by a weighty moan.

I could hear shuffling on the oversized leather recliner followed by the tapping of Momma's heels coming slowly toward me. Justine started quickly turning the pages in the chart. I folded my arms and repositioned myself on the bed.

Momma gently massaged my shoulders with her warm hands. She never said a word, but the message of, "calm down, it's okay," was imparted with every stroke to my tensed body.

Justine continued with her questioning. "Do you consent to receive blood in the event that you need it?"

"Yes."

"Please review this bracelet to ensure that your date of birth is correct."

After a quick look, I confirmed with, "It's correct."

"Okay, if you will extend your arm please, Mrs. Dillard, I'll give you an identification bracelet and a blood product bracelet and we will be all done."

"Thank you."

"Someone from the lab will be in shortly to draw your blood."

I was beyond elated to see Justine close my door. I knew better than to explode on her like I really wanted to, especially since she would be caring for me. I was determined to maintain my composure and not embarrass my momma. However, when the door closed I was at liberty to say exactly what I felt. As a matter of fact, I had been rehearsing my lethally vile since the very moment she asked me how many living children I had.

"Do not even say a word. I know – I heard exactly what she said. She's just doing her job, it's okay. Just think, after this surgery you'll never have to answer that question again."

"You're right Momma, but surely they have to know that women who come here for a cerclage have lost a child or multiple children. So, what is the point of even asking?"

There was a knock at the door and the phlebotomist was at my bedside. "Hi, I'm Annsley. I just need to get a little blood from you today. Can I see your I.D. bracelet please?"

169

"Yes," I nicely replied extending my right hand. "I will warn you, I am a very hard patient to stick. My veins are deep, but this one here on my left arm never lets me down."

"Thanks for the heads up. I hate to stick my patients more than twice. Let's see if I can find this super vein."

Turning my head toward the window, I closed my eyes and patiently waited to hear, "I'm all done." After several pokes, Annsley sincerely apologized. "I'm calling for another lab technician to come draw your blood. I hope you won't have to be stuck much more."

I was not surprised at all. It usually took no less than six attempts for my veins to show up for duty. I knew I was in for a few more rounds of being the pincushion. The second lab technician arrived and gave earnest attempts at finding the perfect spot. After four needle sticks, she gave up and exited the room in search of an electronic vein finder.

The anesthesiologist and her intern came in to review consents and administer the epidural just after twelve thirty. I did not have any questions about the process. Only a silent prayer that this one would pale in comparison to the one proceeding Madison's delivery. They swiftly went through all of the routine questions about allergies, current medications, significant medical conditions and so forth. "No," I quickly answered to each question.

"Any history of blood transfusions?"

"No."

"How many pregnancies?"

Taken aback by the sensitive question, I was immediately infuriated. If my eyes were a knife, they would have cut through every single layer of skin, just as that question cut directly to my heart. "Three!!!...THREE!!!"

"I've had three damn pregnancies and all three of them are dead now!!! All of them!!! Was that your next question, 'How many living children???'"

"Why, tell me, why did I even bother to complete all of this paperwork if you were just going to ask me the same questions again?!"

"Mrs. Dillard, I am so..."

Lifting my hand in disgust, "I do not want to hear any more stupid apologies. The question is just unnecessary. No one has an abdominal cerclage placed without having lost at least one child. The question is just absurd. Women from across the world come here every day because Dr. McDonald has the expertise to place cerclages. He is compassionate – he gets it! Too bad nobody else here does!"

"Tanika, please baby, calm down. She is just doing her job," Momma said squeezing my hand tightly.

My palms were sweating profusely, but Momma refused to let my hand go until I ended my tirade. "Mrs. Dillard, I am sincerely sorry for upsetting you. It was not my intent at all. I am deeply sorry for all of your losses," the anesthesiologist said with tears in her eyes.

"I understand," I replied.

"I'll give you a few minutes with your mom and then I'll come back for your epidural placement. Is that okay?"

"You are fine to place it now. I'm okay. I am just ready to get this started and over."

"She doesn't have her IV yet. There was a problem finding a vein," the intern whispered to the anesthesiologist.

"Mrs. Dillard, we need to get an IV started first. Is it okay if we try?"

"Sure, go ahead."

Both the anesthesiologist and the intern put on gloves and they each searched my arms for a vein. "Let's try this one here," the intern said as she pointed to the exact vein that I mentioned to the lab tech earlier. With one try, they found a vein and were able to start my IV and subsequently place my epidural with no further complications or questions. At last, we were making progress and getting closer to the cerclage placement.

The nurse peeped in my room to announce that Dr. McDonald was on the floor and would be in to greet me in a few moments. My heart began to race at the thought of meeting the man that would change my life and our bloodline. Before I had time to rehearse what I would say to him, he was

171

walking in the door. "Good afternoon, Mrs. Dillard!" he said with a hearty smile. "It's nice to meet you in person."

"Hi, Dr. McDonald, I am so happy to be here."

"I hope your travels here were uneventful, and feel free to call me Dr. H."

"Our travel was perfect. This is my mom, Katherine; she'll be my caregiver while I'm here."

"Your mom?" he asked in dismay. "You ladies could certainly pass for sisters. Nice to meet you also Katherine."

"I heard about you from ladies all over the world who have had miscarriages and come to you for a TAC. Many of them now have rainbow babies."

"You know, I'm always impressed at the power of connection between ladies who have experienced the loss of a baby. There is a common thread of pain, but there is also an equally amazing thread of hope, empowerment, and education that you all share," he replied.

"I totally agree. One of my blog followers from the West Coast urged me to contact you. She's had several second trimester losses and plans to have a TAC one day if she and her husband decide to expand their family."

"That's incredible – absolutely incredible," Dr. McDonald said with amazement. "And don't you worry; you will be one of the mothers who have a rainbow baby. In fact, after today's surgery, you can have all of the children that you want."

"That is good news Dr. McDonald. I've been reminding myself of that since we spoke on the phone."

"Now, do you also recall the surgical process that we discussed via phone several weeks ago?" he asked.

"Yes, I do."

"Well, I've reviewed all of your records from Drs. Laurel and Halton. I want to look for fibroids, because I did see in the notes that you had some with your last pregnancy. I may not have to touch them depending on the location, but we'll just have to wait and see. Now, do you have any questions to ask of me?"

"Just one – how long do we have to wait until we can build our family?"

Dr. McDonald's head began to nod. "Yes, yes, yes! You know, that is the one single question most everyone asks. I am happy to tell you that you and your husband can start trying to conceive in the next thirty days. I generally set those parameters just so you've had one cycle and can adequately date the pregnancy. It will also give your abdominal cavity time to recover."

"Oh, that makes me so happy!"

"It makes me happy too," Momma said. "I'm closer to having more grandkids. Thank you, Mr. McDonald."

"If there are no more questions, we'll get you some good sleeping medicine and then wheel you down to pre-op and get started. Katherine, I will have the nurse show you where the recovery waiting area is. We'll call you as soon as we're done," he instructed.

"Tanika, you're going to be fine. I can guarantee all three of your daughters couldn't be more proud of you. I'm sure that they are cheering you on." What a reassuring thought. Dr. McDonald certainly soothed my anxious heart with his sensitivity and compassion.

Momma hugged me tightly and said a quick prayer. "Please call Chris and update him. I thought that I would have had time to call him, but I didn't."

"I will," she replied.

The nurse came in and hit a few buttons on my IV. "Now, just relax and count with me. We're going to start at one hundred and count down."

In concert, we counted, "100, 99, 98, 97…"

I felt extremely cold, uncomfortable, and annoyed by all of the beeping noises. The bright lights hurt my eyes, so I just kept them closed. "Mrs. Dillard, are you in any pain right now?" she asked in a soft voice whisper.

"Yes, my throat hurts," I murmured as I tried diligently to open my eyes.

"You are in the recovery room. I let your mom know that you are here. She will be able to come back to see you as soon as I get you settled."

"Did I already have the surgery?"

"Yes ma'am."

"That seemed really quick. What time is it?"

"It's close to six o'clock."

"Did he have to go to the mountain?" I asked quietly.

"Pardon me?"

"Never mind," I said drifting back to sleep.

There were phones ringing, people talking loudly. Resting quietly was no longer an option. My frustration and my pain level were equal. I awoke like an angry bear. "Why is everyone acting like this is everything except a recovery room?" I mumbled to myself.

"Well, hello there, Baby Cakes!"

"Hey, Momma, how long have you been here?"

"Over an hour or so. You were sleeping really good, so I didn't want to bother you. How do you feel?"

"Just a little bit sore, but okay otherwise. Did Dr. McDonald find you?"

"He did. He said that the surgery went perfectly and he would see you in the morning when he makes his rounds. Chris called several times to check on you. Do you feel up to talking to him?"

"I most certainly do. It seems like it has been forever since I've spoken to him."

Momma pressed the speed dial for Chris and gave me the phone and he answered before the first ring was complete. "Hello."

"Hey Babe," I excitedly replied.

"I am so glad to hear your voice. How do you feel?"

"Just a little sore, but I should be getting some medicine soon, I hope."

"Well, Momma told me that you did great today and that the surgery went well."

"Yes, Dr. McDonald said I did great, but I haven't seen him yet to get all of the details. I can't speak for you, but I will be ready to try for another baby in thirty days."

"What? Thirty days?" he asked with surprise.

"Absolutely – thirty days. We have waited long enough. It's time to build a family and fill our home with some kids. Do you agree?"

"Yes, but thirty days just seems so soon. It seems like you would have to wait a bit longer since you just had major surgery."

"Nope, Dr. McDonald said just thirty days. And besides, you know I'm tough. I can handle it," I said with a hearty smile.

"I am so happy that this is behind us. I cannot wait for you to get home."

"I agree. I can't wait to be back at home with you. I'll call you tomorrow. The nurse is here with my medicine and I plan to go to sleep, because I am exhausted."

"Okay, good night Babe, I love you!" he said in a rich, soulful voice.

"I love you more. Goodnight."

The nurse informed me that Dr. McDonald came by while I was napping. He did not want to disturb me and opted to see me the following morning when he made his rounds. His decision was perfectly fine with me. I was in no position to hear the account of my surgery at that moment. After a dose of pain medicine was injected to my IV site, I was transported back to my room on the 7th floor where I slept soundly for the remainder of the evening.

Before dawn, I could hear unwelcomed chatter in the hallway. I stretched and tried to adjust my well-rested eyes to see the time on the large clock that hung in front of me. All of the numbers seemed to overlap each other. Thankfully, my cell phone was in arms' reach and I was able to see 6:30 a.m. in the display window.

All of the commotion I heard was the night shift nurses giving report to the new nurses on duty. There was a very soft knock on the door prior to its opening. "Mrs. Dillard."

"Come in."

"Hi, I am Stacey – I'll be taking care of you today. Is there anything that I can get for you right now?"

"No, thank you. I am okay, just a tad bit sore."

"You can have your pain medicine every four to six hours. Would you like more now? It is much easier to stay ahead of the pain rather than try to eliminate it once it has started."

"No, I will wait on the medicine. I want to get up for a hot shower and try to walk around. I think if I could move around, I would feel better."

"That's a great idea. I will go and complete a quick assessment on my other patients, and then I can come back to help you shower. Dr. McDonald is on the floor this morning; it might be wise to wait until he sees you before you get into the shower."

"Sure, I don't want to miss him."

Stacey completed her evaluation of my incision and vital signs. "Hang tight. Dr. McDonald should be here momentarily."

"Do you think I could get the Foley and IV out now? I don't want to get into the shower with them if I do not have to."

"Let me check, the orders are likely already on the chart. I haven't had a chance to review it in detail."

"Oh, I understand. You can just let me know whenever you have a chance."

"No worries, I just found it. We can get rid of both the Foley and the IV as long as you promise to stay hydrated," she explained.

"Yes! I will drink whatever you tell me to."

Stacey grabbed a pair of gloves and gently removed the catheter and the IV. I felt immediate freedom as I stretched both hands above my head.

"Good morning," Momma said in her excited voice.

"Morning Sunshine! How did you sleep?" I asked, still stretching.

"Surprisingly, I slept well in this recliner. I feel like I rested last night."

"Oh yes, I don't know if it was the anesthesia wearing off or complete exhaustion, but I slept pretty good too."

"Are you ready for breakfast?" she asked in her motherly way.

"No, but can you help me get out of this bed? I've been in here long enough."

"Yes ma'am, I can," she responded.

"I want to wash my face and brush my teeth before Dr. McDonald comes in. The nurse said that he's on the floor and should be in soon."

We moved slowly and carefully from the bed to the bathroom. Somehow, my mind and my body we not on the same page or speed for that matter. Nevertheless, we made it to the green, outdated bathroom. Momma held me around the waist in the event that I became unsteady on my feet.

The feel of the scalding hot washcloth on my oily face erased the tension in my neck and shoulders. I savored every minute and anxiously awaited the longest shower of my life as soon as Dr. McDonald made his rounds.

There was a rapid tapping at the door, "Good Morning, Dr. McDonald here."

He was well-groomed, having traded in his scrubs for khaki dress slacks and a linen shirt.

"Not a moment too soon! Good Morning, Dr. H."

"Well, look at you moving around so well."

"I don't know that this is well, but I had to get out of the bed and move around."

"That's exactly what I want you to do. The more that you move, the better you'll feel. So, take a few laps around the unit. Even if you move at a snail's pace, at least you'll be moving your muscles."

"Okay, I can do that."

"Well, I have some good news for you," he said with a wide smile.

"I have been waiting all night to hear the report."

"The TAC placement went well, but I did remove seven fibroids and a cyst from your ovary. Four of those fibroids had attached to your uterine walls. So, all were removed without any problem."

"That's great! Thank you Lord," I said with jubilation.

"Thank you Lord," Momma echoed repeatedly with her hands slightly lifted.

"Now, initially I said that you and Chris would be able to try to conceive in a month. But, because of the fibroid removal, I feel that it is best to advise a three month wait before getting pregnant. You will need time for the uterine walls to heal before a fertilized egg tries to attach there."

My smile quickly faded. "I know that you wanted to build a family right away and I can see the disappointment on your face. But remember, I said that I have good news. The ninety day delay is not bad news at all. How about you and Chris use the next three months to fall in love again, date, and recharge."

"You guys have been through a great deal in the last two and a half years. Take some time for each other. After all, you will not have him solely to yourself for at least the next eighteen years after your next baby comes home," he continued.

"Thank you for helping me to see this differently. Everything you're saying is perfect advice, although slightly different than what I had planned."

"Yes, it's all about perspective. I assure you that this waiting period will be the fastest three months of your life."

"I certainly hope so."

Dr. McDonald reviewed my discharge instructions and the follow up plans for when I returned home to Dr. Halton. I would not be officially released from the hospital until later that afternoon, but he wanted to go over the details ahead of time. "Thank you for everything. I am sure you'll hear from us next year with some exciting news."

"That's exactly what I want to happen, my dear. Remember, I'm just a phone call or an email away. Do not hesitate to contact me," he said patting my shoulder as he left the room.

There was an undeniable energy that overshadowed me. Perhaps a portion of that energy was closure of the pain of pregnancy loss now that the TAC was securely in place. There was also an expectant hope of joy that came with rekindled love and birthed life.

Without assistance, I glided into the sauna-like shower and imagined all of the many things that Chris and I could do to reconnect over the next three months. I closed my eyes, sang our favorite love songs and envisioned cuddling with him by the fire. Then I reminisced of the magic of our first kiss and my stiff legs became weak. I recalled the sound of his velvet voice whispering the inaugural, "I love you," and the electrifying response that pulsated through my body. The intense passion in his light brown eyes flashed before me. Now, I could hardly wait to leave Boston Hospital and return to my lover. But most importantly, I wanted to restore what we had before our losses.

"Are you okay in there?" Momma said in a mildly concerned tone.

"Oh, oh, yes ma'am. I am on my way out now."

I had been in the shower for nearly forty minutes. "Okay, take your time. Son called a few minutes ago. I told him that I would have you call him as soon as you got out of the shower."

"I didn't realize the time. Would you grab my phone for me? I'll call him now before his break is over."

Before I completely dried off, I had called his phone twice, but there was no answer. "Babe, I am so sorry I missed your call. I was in the shower daydreaming about you. Call me when you can. I love you so much."

After my long shower, I got dressed, ate breakfast, and started walking the halls as instructed. My cell phone was in my pants pockets so I would be sure not to miss another call. Dr. McDonald was right, the more that I walked, the better I felt. Nothing was going to hold me back from being well enough to board the plane the next day.

When our plane arrived we were greeted at the airport by the most amazing man – my husband. He was holding half-dozen yellow roses and there were another dozen roses on top of the car. "Hello, my love!!!" I yelled as I walked through the exit doors.

"Welcome home, Momma. These are for you. Thank you for taking care of Babe."

"Oh, thank you son, these are gorgeous," Momma replied giving him a tight hug around the neck.

"There's my Babe. Come here, I have missed you," he said with a kiss.

I didn't need words in that moment. All that I needed was to be found in his strong, yet gentle arms. His soft, warm lips touched mine and time stood still. At last, my heart was at home. "And these are for you," he said as he presented me with the vase of red, long stem roses.

"Oh Christopher, they're beautiful. Thank you."

Momma and I discussed the details of the trip and our hospital stay with Chris. There just wasn't enough time to chat about the minor elements during our brief phone conversation. Occasionally, in the middle of our conversation, I would doze in and out. I was indeed tired and sore from the hustle of traveling, but I was also being lulled to sleep by the scent of his cologne.

Chapter 16
Reconnecting Love

"Babe, what should we do this weekend?"

"Hopefully, I'll feel well enough to put on that sexy red dress you like. We can go to dinner and then downtown to the jazz bar."

"That sounds like a good idea to me," he co-signed cheerfully.

"I agree. We haven't been on a date in a while."

"Are you planning to wear the red dress that you wore to the company Christmas party last year?"

"Yes sir, that red dress," I replied as I kissed his shiny, bald head.

"If you wear that dress, I'm not certain that we'll make it through dinner," he said with a mischievous smile. "I am stuck to you like a magnet when you wear that dress."

"Oh believe me; we will make it through dinner. Don't get any elaborate ideas just yet. I am still a bit sore from the surgery."

Chris put his index finger on my lips. "You just focus on your recovery and I will take care of everything else, okay?" he said as he gently kissed my cheek and walked away.

Calling him back for more was my intention. However, I was enamored and speechless by the power of his words and his touch. "Focus on recovery, focus on recovery!" echoed through my head.

I needed and wanted to be well, especially for our date. I tossed my comfortable flip flops back into the closet and exchanged them for walking shoes. With the CD player loaded with love songs from the eighties, I carefully climbed on the treadmill. Surprisingly, I had walked a slow mile in twenty minutes. My walk was more like a rhythmic stroll, with intentional pauses to join in singing my favorite tunes.

"Are you supposed to be exercising yet?"

"Yeah, Dr. H. said he wants me to move so my abdominal muscles don't tighten and cause more pain. I'm just about finished."

"Okay, I just don't want you trying to do too much too fast," Chris commented with concern.

"I'm going to shower and then rest until it's time to go downtown. What time are we leaving?"

"Six o'clock."

A quick shower followed by a nap on the couch made for a delightful afternoon. I was awakened by a firm nudge on my shoulder. "It's time to get up. We don't want to be late."

I hurriedly went to the bathroom mirror to pin my hair up, apply my makeup, and put on the same jewelry that I wore for our wedding day. The hair brush turned into a microphone as I bellowed more love songs. I slipped into the silk, one-shouldered, red dress and slowly twirled to make sure everything was in its perfect place.

"Oh Wow! Look at you. You look amazing," Chris said as he gently kissed my neck and exposed shoulder.

"Thanks Babe. I feel pretty amazing too. Almost like the same way I felt on our first date to Journey's. Do you remember that?"

"Yes, but I couldn't do this on our first date," he said pressing his body firmly against mine, pinning me to the wall. We had kissed thousands of times over the years, but that passionate exchange was by far the most exhilarating of all.

"We don't have to go to dinner or the show if you don't want to leave," he said.

Maneuvering my way from his love grip, I laughingly expressed, "No sir, we are getting out of here now before this nice dress is on the floor."

Despite our best efforts to arrive on time for the six thirty dinner reservations, we were twenty minutes late. Pleasure temporarily detained us and we did not mind. Thankfully, the restaurant was less crowded than usual and we were able to be seated in an oversized, leather booth without delay. "Slide on over, please."

"What are you doing?" I asked.

"I'm sitting beside you tonight. I will feel too far away from you sitting across the table," he said.

We were quite cozy as we reviewed the menu and ordered dinner. By the time our food arrived, I was intoxicated off of love and barely ate my bourbon glazed salmon and asparagus. Chris on the other hand, had no problem making his prime rib, salad and baked potato disappear. Even with our late start, we were on time for the jazz performance in the dimly lit, rustic music hall.

Our bodies swayed to the rhythm of those harmonious sounds. I wanted to get out of my seat, wrap my arms around his neck and dance. But, Chris is much too modest for public dancing. However, to his delight, there was not a dance floor in the music hall. "Can we go outside for a minute?"

"What's wrong? Do you feel sick?" he asked with heightened concern.

"No, I feel fine. I just want to go outside. We will still be able to hear the music."

"Okay, if that's what you want," he responded with uncertainty.

Chris grabbed my hand and we maneuvered through the crowd to the exit doors. "It feels so nice out here. It's much warmer than expected, certainly doesn't feel like fall weather to me."

"Yeah, it feels more like a warm, summer evening. Can we dance?" I asked.

"Out here? Do you mean right now?"

"Yes, can we dance right here on the sidewalk right now?" I replied.

We both laughed, partly at the ridiculous request and partly at the thought of someone seeing us. To my surprise, there was no rebuttal--only immediate action. Before I could finish my girlish giggles, his arm was securely around my waist and we were gliding from left to right. My heart nearly leaped out of my chest with excitement. The last time that we danced other than at home was at our wedding reception three years prior. "We can just dance to this song and then go back inside," I whispered in his ear.

"No, no – we can stay here as long as you'd like."

I wanted to back away to make sure that it really was my husband. Nothing about his words or actions reflected the Chris that I knew. Rather than talk, I deposited soft kisses on his cheek and gently scratched his back. Nearly twenty minutes had passed without us saying a word. We were rhythmically, physically, mentally, and emotionally in sync. Nothing mattered in those moments but us. We were so focused on each other that we couldn't recall if others walked by or if we heard the noise of cars driving down the street.

"Are you ready to go back inside?" Chris asked.

"The show is close to the end. It's almost eleven o'clock. I'm fine if we head home," I responded.

"I don't want the night to end."

"It doesn't have to," I said holding his hand.

We walked hand in hand down Main Street until we arrived at our car and after several passionate kisses we headed home. Dr. McDonald was majestically precise in his suggestion to reconnect and to date again. We are so grateful that we followed the doctor's orders.

Chapter 17
Wisdom Speaks

"*Is there anything that you need to tell me?*" was the text message that displayed on my mobile phone from Summer. We had worked together for nine years before Summer moved to another office. Our relationship as coworkers had evolved into a friendship with a connection like a family. She and her husband Joe were my role models. They were young lovers who had been married over twenty years. They embodied values of faith, hard work, and fun.

"*Today is Destiny's second birthday in heaven. I'm laying on the couch thinking about how life would be with her, but I am not sad,*" I replied,

"*Is there anything else you need to tell me?*" Summer quickly responded.

I thought intently about what Summer could be alluding to with her repeated question. Nothing new was happening in the office. It was not a birthday or anniversary day for them; therefore, I replied, "Honestly Summer, nothing. What did I forget?"

"I don't want this to upset you, but I just had a dream about you."

I read the message and immediately dialed her number. She had dreams about me before and they were vivid and accurate. "Hello," she answered.

"Hey, I assumed that the conversation would be too detailed for text messages. What are you dreaming about?"

"Tanika, I just had a dream so real that it brought tears to my eyes."

"Really? What happened?"

"Joe and I were taking a nap, but I started dreaming that we went to the hospital. I came in the room and you placed the most beautiful baby boy in my arms. Tanika, he had jet black, silky hair and smelled so good. It was that clean, lavender sent on him that I smelled. I was literally holding him."

"Oh Summer!" I said with a lump in my throat.

"I woke Joe up from his nap and asked him where was the baby and if he could smell lavender lotion. He thought I was absolutely crazy, Tanika."

I laughed at the visualization of Joe waking up from a nap with strange questions. "Summer, what did he say? I would have thought you were crazy too."

"He asked me what the heck I was talking about and whose baby has been here?"

"I had to tell him the whole dream and was in tears by the end. Tanika, I have never had a dream so real in my entire life. Joe thought that it might upset you if I told you, but I just couldn't keep it inside. I feel like God was showing me what is coming."

"Oh Summer, one day it will be true. And believe me; it does not upset me at all. I know that God speaks to you through dreams, just like He did with my Grandma."

"Remember, you had a dream about someone being pregnant just a few days before I found out I was carrying Briauna? I know that I am not pregnant right now, but maybe this is the sign that we are ready to try even though we are few weeks shy of the three month waiting period. I can't wait to tell Chris about your dream. Thank you so much for sharing this."

"Alright sister, you and Chris go have fun. Don't stop until you have my little nephew," Summer said with a hearty laugh as we ended the call.

As I told Chris every detail of the dream, his eyes lit up as bright as the lights on our Christmas tree. "Wow that is an incredible dream. What are you thinking?"

"I am excited that this will soon be a reality and no longer something that we have only in our sleep and imagination."

"I agree."

Chris gathered some art supplies from the shelf and asked, "Are you ready to make her card?"

"Yes, I'm ready."

We each created a special birthday card to acknowledge and celebrate our little princess. My card was filled with glittery butterflies and a poem. Chris made a card with red hearts and heartwarming sentiments. Our craft session concluded with placing the cards in Madison's Christmas stocking and reading a scripture about faith. I made myself comfortable on the couch with my favorite fleece blanket with hopes of seeing our son or anything comparable to Summer's dream.

Perhaps my anticipation was greater than my fatigue, because I could not fall asleep. I cradled the stomach that had held life three times before. My mind slowly daydreamed about hearing the heartbeat and feeling the flutters of existence again. As much as I wanted to focus on the future, I could not escape my past.

Destiny weighed heavily on my mind and even more on my heart. We should have been hosting a huge birthday party for our two year old daughter. I stood in the guest room and looked on the top shelf at the purple memory box, which actually held very few memories. Somehow seeing the twenty-three chromosomes on the pathology report validated her existence. I read through the sympathy cards and had a good cry. "That's enough crying. You still have so much more life inside of you. Get up."

I looked around the room and everything was still. No one had joined me, but I sensed that I wasn't the only person in the room. I quickly glanced behind me and then above my head, but I was alone. "Get up!" the voice echoed gently.

I squared my shoulders and abruptly placed the memory box back onto the shelf. "Now what?" I asked as I threw my hands up and searched for a face to accompany the voice that spoke to me. There was no response. I exited the room, closed the door behind me, and stood at the kitchen window.

It was a beautiful, unusually warm day without a cloud in the sky. My foot gently tapped the floor and I started singing Grandma's music about trusting God. The more I sang, the more I sensed a faceless presence and heard a familiar voice again. The music had transformed my temporary sorrow to an expectant hope. "Grandma?" I said with a smile as I circled my kitchen. "It is you!"

How my heart leaped for joy at the thought of Grandma being furloughed from heaven to encourage me. She never uttered another word, but her spirit encompassed our home like a tender breeze. The kid in me was revived. I snuggled up to her on the couch and rested my head in her lap. Her soft, wrinkled hands ran through my hair just as they did on countless occasions before. "Did you come to tell me something?"

There was no reply even after an extended delay. "Okay, what about my girls? What do you think of them, Grandma?"

Again, there was silence; however, there was a deep chill that came over me. I wanted to hear stories about my daughters and who they were most similar to in appearance and behavior. I longed to hear her proclaim her love and affection for them. I knew that she spoiled them, but I wanted to hear the elaborate details. She was my lifeline to heaven and the only one who could perfectly paint the picture that I desperately wanted to see.

After a couple more unanswered questions, I realized that she had said all she needed to say. I had to be okay with her decision. I closed my eyes, calmed the countless thoughts in my head and simply savored every second of her angelic presence. "My goodness, what time is it?" I said mid-yawn.

I realized that Grandma had made her departure back to her eternal home as I slept upon her lap. It was likely for the best that our visit ended so peacefully. I got up as she instructed me to do. My attitude was more optimistic and there was an unexplainable excitement knowing that there was still life and *new* life within me.

Our weekend followed the traditional pattern: a dinner date on Saturday followed by church on Sunday and then an afternoon nap. We cuddled, talked about our plans for Christmas Day and last-minute gifts to pick up. "What do you want for Christmas?" Chris asked.

"A baby" I replied frankly.

"Well, what do you want for your birthday?"

"My birthday? A baby," I replied in the same tone which followed a hearty laugh since my birthday was so far away.

"No seriously, what do you want that I can purchase from a store?" he emphasized.

"Nothing at all. I don't need any more possessions."

"What about you, what do you want?" I asked.

"Nothing – I don't need anything either."

Laying in silence, we considered how thankful we were not to be in need or in greed. We counted all of the plentiful blessings that had been entrusted to us. Just as my eyes closed for our long-awaited nap, His strong arm gripped tighter around my waist. "You look amazingly beautiful today."

"Thank you, Babe," I said with a girlish grin.

"No, there was something unique about your eyes today."

"Really? I didn't do anything different with my makeup. What did you see?"

"It was almost as if I could see through your eyes and into your soul. I can't quite put it into words."

"Let me turn around so that you can look at them again. Tell me more."

Our eyes met passionately and intently as we gazed at each other. Without warning or verbal invitation, our bodies moved closer. We breathed the same breath. He was so near to me that I felt the rapid beating of his heart. He moved closer until there was no space between us. We were one: in mind, in purpose, and in love. That was the first Sunday in ages that we had missed our afternoon nap. However, it was an unforgettable experience that I would happily repeat on any day of the week.

The remainder of the month seemed to go by rapidly. Christmas was remarkably better than the past two years. We didn't give or receive expensive gifts or travel abroad; we simply changed our perspective and celebrated the real reason for the season.

Blog Update: December 31, 2009

I really wanted to bypass the Christmas season altogether and go straight into the New Year. There were so many milestones in December. I knew this would be an emotional month and I just didn't want to deal with it.
   • ***Milestone 1**: Destiny's 2nd angel birthday on December 19th.*
   • ***Milestone 2**: Madison's due date on December 22nd.*
   • ***Milestone 3**: Briauna's due date on December 28th.*

Now, do you see why I wanted to jump into January? I had already prepared myself to get the sackcloth and ashes and basically be miserable for thirty-one days. I had anticipatory depression and panic attacks. Thankfully, the Lord spoke to me and reminded me that I had control over my emotions and that I could command the day with good thoughts. 'How so?' I wondered.

I counted the number of days between milestones 1 and 3 and decided that we'd have a theme for each day. The theme would be our prayer focus and include a coordinating scripture to go along with it. On the milestone day, we'd recognize each daughter by making a card, writing a letter or any creative activity that we'd come up with. We called this time, "Ten Days of Remembrance & Prayer."

Day 1: *Saturday, December 19th*
Destiny & Faith – Hebrews 11:6.

Day 2: *Sunday, December 20th*
Healing – Exodus 15:26.

Day 3: *Monday, December 21st*
Joy – Nehemiah 8:9-12.

Day 4: *Tuesday, December 22nd*
Madison & Hope – 1 Tim 4:8-11

Day 5: *Wednesday, December 23rd*
Friends – John 15:15

Day 6: *Thursday, December 24th*
Family

Day 7: *Friday, December 25th*
Jesus Christ – Isaiah 9

Day 8: *Saturday, December 26th*
New Beginnings – Isaiah 43:19

Day 9: *Sunday, December 27th*
Thanksgiving – 1 Chronicles 16:8

Day 10: *Monday, December 28th*
Briauna & Love – 1 Corinthians 13

Thankfully, this plan worked for us. We were able to get our minds off of the grief and were mindful of God's word and His promises to us. We definitely have a new tradition. The best part about this was making our cards for the girls. Chris and I each made a card for each girl, shared our thoughts with each other, and put the card in the Christmas stocking. We plan to make new cards each year. I'll have to admit that this was the first Christmas since 2007 that we really had peace, hope, and joy.

Chapter 18
The Most Wonderful Time of the Year

Our lives quickly normalized after an event-filled holiday season. Having our lazy Saturday afternoons back was a welcomed change of pace. The hustle and bustle of Christmas parties, dinner dates, shopping, and family gatherings had given me a renewed appreciation for the simple things on my to-do list like grocery shopping.

The small town grocery store was filled with good sales and even better conversation. It was extremely rare to go to Maude's Market and not encounter someone you knew. Just as I was headed to the bakery, I saw Mrs. Anderson. She lived a few doors down from my cousins and used to teach home economics at my school. "Hey, Mrs. Anderson, it's good to see you."

"Hey, Darling, it's good to see you too. How are you doing?"

"I'm fine. How are you?"

"I reckon I am alright. Any day above ground is a good day," she chuckled. "Now, how is the baby doing?"

"We don't have any kids right now Mrs. Anderson," I answered.

"You don't? The last time that I talked to your uncle, he told me that you were pregnant again and doing just fine this time."

"Yes Ma'am, but she passed away in July."

Mrs. Anderson shook her head regretfully and said, "Oh honey, I am so sorry. I had no idea. I..."

Quickly interrupting before more unnecessary words spewed from her lips, "It's okay, Mrs. Anderson. You didn't know."

"So, you all have tried again I see."

As she leaned in, opened my leather jacket and inspected my stomach. "No ma'am, I am not pregnant!"

"Well, you are certainly glowing like you are. I think you are fooling me. You'd better be sure."

"I need to finish my shopping and head home. Take care, Mrs. Anderson."

"You do the same," she said in a slow, confused tone.

The shopping cart was on two wheels as I made a u-turn and went directly to the checkout counter. I couldn't run the risk of talking to anyone else in the store. So, Chris's only requested item, vanilla bean ice cream, could not be filled – at least not that day. Surprisingly, not a single tear was shed. *'The nerve of people to ask such personal questions,'* I said to myself in disbelief.

After unloading the groceries into the trunk, I sat in the car and replayed the entire conversation with Mrs. Anderson. I laughed at the unfiltered frankness of her comments and inquires. Maybe that is just the way older people are. They say exactly what they think without much thought. Just as I turned the key in the ignition, I saw Mrs. Anderson exit the store and proceed to her car. I waited until she was on the highway before going back into the store for Chris's ice cream.

My car wouldn't move fast enough back to our house so that I could inform Chris of what happened. "Babe, you will not believe what Mrs. Harriett Anderson said to me in the store!"

Chris folded his arms and listened intently as I dramatically explained the dialogue. He never showed any emotion or any expression to indicate how he felt. "I am still trying to get over the fact that she asked me if I was pregnant. That is not something that you ask people. You wait for an announcement to be made. I know she's old, but she should know better," I said placing the ice cream on the counter.

"Babe, in the big picture, it doesn't matter what she said. You have to be responsible for how you respond. You have given her the power to control your emotions with her words. You have to calm down."

Chris always gave sound advice in a loving way that was easy to receive. "Now that you put this in perspective for me, I am ending this discussion and regaining command of my emotions. Thank you."

"I do want to ask you a question."

"Sure, what is it? Ask me anything," I anxiously replied.

"Are you pregnant?"

An immediate and emphatic "No" burst from my lips. "What made you ask?"

"I've just noticed a few small changes over the last few days that made me wonder."

Gently interrupting, "Changes like what?"

"Today when you were ironing your jeans, I was looking at you from the side. I am almost certain that I saw a protruding stomach."

"Really? What else have you noticed?"

"Your face is brighter, almost as if it has a glow to it. And you have eaten almost a whole jar of pickles."

Feeling all over my face as if to sense the glow that he and Mrs. Anderson had been able to view, I couldn't appreciate what they saw. I rushed into the guest bathroom and closely inspected my reflection. My eyes looked normal. My nose was oily, but otherwise, I only saw my non-glowing face. The side view in the mirror raised a slight suspicion. My thumb rested just below my bra line as my hands met to form a heart shape upon my stomach. "Can this be true?" I wondered.

"Babe, come here!"

Rushing up the hallway, Chris yelled, "What's wrong?"

"Look at this stomach. What do you think?" I asked as I called his attention on my side profile.

"You look pregnant to me," he said with certainty. "Do you have any pregnancy tests here?"

"I may have one of the cheap ones left over from last year. If we have any, I will wait to test first thing in the morning for the most accurate results."

"I can already tell you that it will be positive. Let's just go buy a digital test so that we can know now," he suggested.

With confidence, I uttered, "No, we can wait until tomorrow," as I rubbed my stomach and hoped for the best.

Surprisingly, we made it through the night without even mentioning the possibility of pregnancy or taking the test. Just before dawn on Sunday morning, I gathered my supplies from the bathroom cabinet and tested. My heart bounded out of my chest and tiny beads of sweat were on my forehead as I watched the white test strip turn pink. I saw the control line and anxiously waited to see another line to confirm a positive test.

After what seemed like five minutes, I did not see any indication of the result line turning pink. I read the instructions on the test box again, just to be certain that I had waited long enough. In fact, I had waited more than the full three minutes that were required. My chest contoured inwardly as I released a sigh of frustration. The test was negative.

I returned to bed and lay with my back away from Chris. Warm tears fell from my eyes and across the bridge of my nose. I was disappointed with the test results, but I didn't want Chris to know. He was certain that we would have a positive test. How was I going to tell him differently?

The tear stained sheet revealed that something was going on. "Morning," he said in a raspy, scratchy voice.

"Morning."

"Why are you crying?" he asked gently.

The right words escaped me. Phrases like, "I'm not pregnant. I'm sorry to disappoint you," and "nothing," were the choices that almost passed through my lips.

Before I could give the best answer, he asked again, "Babe, what is going on? Why are you crying?"

He pulled me closer to him and firmly held his hand to my waist. My chest trembled as I fought back an outburst of tears. "Did you take the test?"

"Yes."

"So, what is the result?"

I shook my head "no" and buried my face in the pillow to muffle the sound of my lamenting.

"Oh Babe, it's okay. This just means that we get to keep trying and there is nothing wrong with that. It will happen just as it has before and probably when we least expect it. We are not giving up though."

"You're right, we're not."

Somehow his strength and optimism disarmed my disappointment and settled my emotional tantrum. We went to church and heard a message about faith that encouraged us to believe that the plan that God designed for our lives would be beneficial for us. The part of the message that we most identified with was, *"even if there were disappointments along the path to our destiny, it makes us appreciate the journey even more."*

We followed our Sunday routine and both were ready for the Sunday afternoon nap. I washed all the makeup from my face and tossed the facial cleaning pad in the trash, but it fell to the floor. I kneeled to the floor to pick up the trash and noticed something odd. The test that I took earlier was in the trash, just as I left it before, but I could see two lines.

Without hesitation, I retrieved the test strip for close inspection. There were clearly two lines on the test: a control line and a faint positive line. "Babe, come here now!!!"

"What is it?" he said as he entered the bathroom.

"Look at this!"

With raised brow, he said, "I see two lines. Did you just take this one?"

"No, it's the same test from this morning. I don't have any more tests here."

"So, it looks like we really are pregnant," he exclaimed.

"Maybe, I'm just confused. I looked at this test for at least five minutes and this line was not there at all. If I am pregnant, why did this line not show up the first time? Do you think the test is old since I've had it for over a year?"

"Is there an expiration date on the box?" Chris inquired.

I pulled the box from the garbage can, "It's good until January of next year."

"We just need to go buy a good digital test and not use these cheap things. That's the only way that you'll believe it. I already know that you are. Do you want to go now or later?"

"We can go after our nap. I'm not going to test until tomorrow morning anyway since that's when you get the most accurate results."

As soon as my head hit the pillow, I was fast asleep. Three hours later I woke up to the aroma of fried chicken. I found Chris in his comfy chair reading the Sunday paper. "How long have you been up?"

"I couldn't sleep. I laid down with you until your snoring drove me out of the room," he chuckled.

"I'm, sorry. You should have told me to turn over."

"I did, but you didn't hear me. It's okay though. I just went to the store and started dinner for us. It's actually ready, except for the brownies for dessert. You can make those since mine never turn out as moist as yours."

"Okay, I can make them after we eat. This is a real treat for you to cook a full Sunday dinner without my assistance."

"I just figured that you needed a break. You seemed so tired."

"Thanks kiddo," I said, placing a soft kiss on his bald head.

"Are you ready to eat now?" he asked.

"Yes, let me go wash my face and hands. I'll make the plates."

Chris had obviously been to more than the grocery store. There were two digital tests on my bathroom counter. One had already been taken out of the package and included a simple note; "Take me!"

His sense of humor and restrained excitement tickled my heart. "Christopher, come here!!!" I yelled just as I started taking the test.

The boyish grin on his face when he peeked around the corner was priceless. "You get to read the results since you wanted this test so badly, Sir. Here you go. It should beep when the result appears in the window."

We waited in silence to hear the magic word. "What?"

"Not pregnant?" Chris said with an astonished look on his face.

"Let me see it. Are you serious?" I asked, grabbing the test from his hands.

"Yes, it says not pregnant," he emphasized.

"I am so confused. Either the second line on the first test is an evaporation line or maybe I am pregnant and it's just too early to tell on the digital test. I don't know. My cycle is supposed to start on Tuesday. I'll get excited when it doesn't come."

During my lunch break on Monday, I purchased four more cheap tests. I needed to know beyond a shadow of a doubt what the true results were. As soon as I walked in the door from work, I took the test. After three minutes, there was a very faint second line which was just a tad darker than the test from Sunday.

Before sunrise on Tuesday morning, I was in the bathroom checking for any sign of my cycle, but there was no sign. The only way to bring my racing thoughts to a halt was to take another cheap test, which was identical to the previous cheap tests. While I wanted to believe the results, the faint lines were not convincing to me.

Wednesday morning, I repeated the testing routine with the fifth test. Surprisingly, the two lines appeared right away. I grabbed the digital test from the vanity just to confirm the results. The magic word quickly appeared in the test window; "PREGNANT."

With a racing heart, sweaty palms, and a lump in my throat, I eased back into the bed beside Chris and eagerly waited for his 5:15 alarm to sound. He bolted out of his sleep at the obnoxious beeping noise. "Good morning, Daddy."

In the midst of a bear-like yawn and stretch, he replied, "Good Morning," followed by a brief pause. "What did you say?"

"I said, Good morning, Daddy!"

"Daddy?" he questioned.

"Yes, you are a Daddy. I took another test thirty minutes ago."

"I knew it!!! I knew it!!!" he cheered with excitement. "When are you calling Dr. Laurel?"

"Today or tomorrow. I just need time for this to settle in my brain. After taking six tests with questionable results, we finally know the truth. Those cheap tests were right all along."

"Actually, I was right from the very start for the record," he commented.

I snapped a picture of the positive test and sent it to Maxine with a personal message to celebrate her birthday. My phone rang immediately. "Oh my goodness, Tee! Congratulations!!!" she screamed. "You know that I am such a crybaby. I need to be forewarned when there is news like this."

Maxine toggled between being the supportive cousin and my long distance OB. She meticulously asked the pertinent questions that any doctor would ask. She also ensured that I made an appointment for lab work within the coming forty-eight hours. "Tee, you have made my birthday extra special. Thank you!"

The authenticity of the positive test was realized by Thursday afternoon. Echoing in my ear were the words of the doctor that changed the course of our family by saying, "You and Chris can have all of the kids that you want." I called Dr. Laurel's office and was instructed to come in Friday morning for a routine blood draw and labs. We opted to keep the news to ourselves until we had the confirmed results from the doctor.

The weekend crawled by as we anxiously awaited the results on Monday. Our weekend calendar was filled with events and we were surrounded by family. I closely examined every article of black clothing that I wore to ensure no one would notice our news and thankfully, no one did.

The long awaited call came from the office on Monday, just after eight o'clock. "So, did you jump out of bed and take a test?" Anne asked with a hearty laugh.

"What are you talking about Anne?"

"Well, your test is positive, but just barely."

"What does that mean?"

"Your HcG is almost eight hundred. It just means that you tested really early, which is fine. Based on this number you are likely three weeks pregnant."

"Oh, I am okay with that. I thought something was wrong."

"Oh no Honey, I didn't mean to alarm you at all. Dr. Laurel does want to repeat the test to ensure that your numbers are increasing appropriately. Can you stop by today?"

"Sure, I can be there within the hour."

"After we get the results back, we'll get you in for an ultrasound. We are going to monitor you like a hawk, so get ready. We all want this so much for you and Chris."

"That's not a problem for me. Chris and I will both appreciate the close observation with this pregnancy."

"Well, congratulations, we will see you soon."

Everything turned out to be perfectly normal with the repeat labs and the ultrasound. Chris and I saw the tiniest miracle of life on the monitor and instantly our hearts were knitted with deep love and affection for our baby. Anne printed an ultrasound picture for our baby book and we held it tightly like a winning lottery ticket. As soon as we made it to the car, we called our mothers to proclaim the news. We shouted in concert, "Hello, Grandma."

They both immediately understood what we were implying. After loud screams, Momma shouted, "When is my baby coming?!"

"It looks like Tanika may be in the hospital for her birthday since the baby is due on the twelfth of September."

The laughter, excitement and screams were the responses from each family member and friend that we called. Thankfully, Chris had the day off and I had taken the day off because I knew I would not be productive after seeing our little miracle for the first time.

One of the most exciting phone calls that day was to Summer. I called her work number and she answered abruptly. "Why are you not at work? Is everything okay?"

"Summer, calm down. Can I not take a day off if I want to?"

"No ma'am, not in the middle of the week. You never do this. Do you have anything to tell me yet?"

"As a matter of fact, I called to say that you were right. Now, there! I said it."

"Yes!" she shouted. "I knew that my dream was just a preview of what was coming. I cannot wait to tell Joe this. So, when is *he* due?" she emphasized.

"He or she is due in September. This also means that based on my calculations, this baby was conceived the very next day after you called to share your dream with me."

There was complete silence on the phone line. "Hello. Summer, are you there?"

"I am here just trying to contain my tears and my excitement in this office. I know what I saw, girlfriend. This baby boy is coming home and I need for you and Chris to believe that. I can't wait to call Joe and tell him this news. He is going to be in tears. You know how emotional he is."

"We are going to choose to believe that this is our miracle baby. Surely, after the surgery, we are never going to experience pregnancy loss again." Summer's friendship and her faith were refreshing. She was certain of our future that included a bright, beautiful son.

The news of our pregnancy spread like wildfire. We shared the news and ultrasound pictures on social media and my blog. My winter wardrobe was immediately switched to maternity clothes. I looked fabulous, I felt amazing, and I was *the* happiest pregnant woman that I knew.

Chris and I both were glowing with excitement and it was unquestionably contagious to all of those whom we encountered. Most everyone shared in our joy, but there were some comments that were inconspicuously pessimistic. "I hope things work out this time," and "this baby will be fine."

On the surface, they appeared to be harmless comments. However the words, *"this time"* and *"this baby,"* stung like a colony of angry bees. I didn't want people to consider our past at all, but view this fourth pregnancy as a totally new, unique experience. The fate of Destiny, Briauna, and Madison had nothing--*absolutely nothing*--to do with the budding miracle that was growing inside of me.

The intended reassurance that *"this baby"* would be fine implied that something was wrong with our other kids. On the contrary, our daughters were perfect in every way; it was my body that had repeatedly failed them. Opting to refrain from an educational exchange on what not to say to expectant families, a forced smile and "thank you," proved to be the most suitable response.

The morning of the gender ultrasound started with a simple email to Lauren, Dominique and Tenille. "Girls, I'm nervous!"

"What's going on TeTe?" Tenille immediately replied to the group.

"The ultrasound is in twenty minutes and I'm more nervous than excited. Surely everything is fine. He/she has been in a knot and rolling around all morning. I'm just nervous about how we'll respond. You wouldn't be surprised if I told you that I'm already crying?"

"Oh don't be nervous, he is going to be swimming around and flashing y'all with all his glory! It will be fine. Deep breath for you and big hug from me. Chris will be holding your hand, you both will cry at the great news and then you'll let everyone know it is a ... BOY!!!! Love ya!" Lauren's words came to life as I envisioned what she said.

Tenille echoed Lauren's thoughts and hurried me along. "Now, get out of the office and go see our niece or nephew. Let us know as soon as possible. All of my co-workers are asking me what "we" are having," she laughed.

Chris was waiting for me in the parking lot at Dr. Halton's office. He was frankly unimpressed that I had made the commute in less than three minutes. He was more concerned that I was two minutes late for the appointment. With no time for a lecture, we checked in with Janice and grabbed a magazine until our name was called. "So today is the big day, right?" she asked.

"Yes, and we cannot wait to finally put all of the assumptions to rest," Chris said with smile.

"Well, I am going to say that we are having a boy. This is just boy season around here," Janice announced.

"You and everyone else are thinking alike on the gender. We will see in just a few moments," I commented.

"Hey friends!" Krista said as she opened the door. "Come on back. I'm ready to see this baby."

We made our usual exchange to talk about our families and current events while she set up the CD for pictures and DVD for a video of the ultrasound. Krista began the exam and effortlessly scanned the baby and simultaneously operated her keyboard without error. We heard the galloping heartbeat and saw all of the major organs. Everything was precisely as we had hoped – unchanged and perfect.

"Alight friends; let's see what this little baby is."

Chris grabbed my hand and we gripped tightly as we gazed at the screen. "Here is a leg and here is the other leg here."

"Is that a hand?" I interjected loudly while leaning forward from the exam table for a closer look.

Krista laughed and shook her head. "Yes ma'am, it is. Can you see what this baby is?"

"Babe, we are having a boy!!!" I screamed. "And oh my goodness, he's showing off his man parts to us."

Chris planted a kiss on my cheek, arose from his seat and started clapping. "That's my boy, that's *my* boy!" Chris said proudly. "Thank you, Lord!"

There was an indescribable, undeniable amazement on his face again. Those glistening, beautiful brown eyes were fixed on the flat screen monitor in front of us. "Now, Christopher Ethan, stop playing with your little toy!" I lovingly commanded.

"I am sorry to tell you, but he'll likely play with that toy for a long time. Trust me," Krista said. "He already has a name?"

"Oh yes, we've had this name picked for some time now. I wanted to honor Chris by naming our first son after him. He's an incredible man and I want our son to be proud to have his father's name," I explained.

"That's so special. Will he be called, "Junior" or "Chris?" Krista asked.

After a hearty laugh, "Neither!" Chris replied. "We're calling him Ethan. We are not passing on my middle name to him, but our initials will be the same. I want him to have his own identity."

Krista finished the scan and took us to the room to consult with Dr. Halton. He was happy and his beautiful blue eyes lit up like the spring sky. We reviewed the follow-up plans and were released for two weeks.

As soon as I arrived back to work, I sent out the long awaited news by email and informed my co-workers. "Here's to announcing with pride and joy, we're expecting a bouncing baby boy! Christopher Ethan is due September 12th."

My phone rang non-stop for the remainder of the day, my inbox was rapidly reaching maximum capacity and my office was constantly filled with well wishers. There were little to no assignments completed on my to-do list that day.

Lauren bubbled over with laughter and yelled, "I told you, I told you!!! I just knew that you were having a boy. My co-workers send their congratulations and well wishes. They are just as excited as I am."

I seemed to skip like a school girl out of the office. The confidence that I felt within me was unmatched by anything I'd ever felt before. My heart soared as I imagined my son being held by Chris, who immediately loved him from the moment his existence was known.

As I drove home, I welcomed every minor traffic jam and red light. The intermittent pauses gave me time to put my hands on my growing belly and speak to Ethan. "Hey Lil' Buddy! Do you know how much Mommy loves you? Daddy and I can't wait to see you in a few months. You are loved by so many people all over the world. Your precious life will cause others to believe in miracles and hope again. Did you know that? We are so honored that we were chosen to be your parents."

My conversations with Ethan became one of the most important parts of my day. The morning commute to work was our time. Feeling his strong kicks targeting my left rib cage his "good morning" message to me. Using the pad of my fingers, we'd play a quick game of tickle the toes as my "good morning" message back to him. He'd hear of our plans for the day and special instructions to show us his face if we had an ultrasound scheduled with Dr. Halton.

Prayers of thanksgiving and songs of praise filled his ears and my heart. Perhaps the pregnancy hormones were the culprit for the steady stream of tears that started each time I spoke to Ethan. Either way, I didn't mind crying happy tears. We were experiencing something new.

The conversations that Chris had with Ethan became the highlight of my night. He was completely connected to our son. "Watch this," he whispered as he tip toed towards my stomach.

He slowly placed both hands on Ethan and rubbed in a circular motion. Within seconds, our little kick boxer was awake, excited to feel his Daddy's hands and welcome him home from work. "Do you feel it today?" I inquired.

Pausing for deep concentration, he replied, "Nope. Nothing today, but he knows it's Dada and that's all that matters."

"Yes, he certainly does. I can't wait for you to feel this too."

Before falling asleep for the night Chris would read a story or Bible verses to Ethan, often asking, "Are you listening Buddy?"

I knew he was because I felt it. His routine concluded with singing the ABC's and a bedtime prayer. "You know we have to start teaching him things early. He's going to be smart. We can't wait until he's two or three to start educating him."

"Yes, I understand and completely agree. He'll be smart-- I'm not worried. He has good genes; he'll be a natural whiz kid, just like me," I said as I kissed his face and found my comfortable spot in the bed.

We planned for a nursery, maternity photos, baby showers, baby dedications, first birthday, graduation, wedding, growing old and becoming grandparents. It was a new level of love and excitement that we had not known before. We were certain that our plans would be more than elaborate thoughts in our head. Dr. McDonald's word and statistics backed up the fact that we really could have all the children we wanted.

The biggest task was merging our individual plans into one that we could both agree on. I envisioned a modern, designer nursery decorated in pastel blue and green, with khaki/brown accents and his name on the wall. Chris refused to have his baby boy in a room with the color green. He said it was too feminine. He wanted a sports nursery with each wall uniquely designed for football, baseball, basketball, and soccer. Thankfully, we compromised and were happy with a jungle-themed nursery. Each letter of Ethan's name was painted with a vibrant orange, calm blue, and a masculine green. The colorful, wooden lion and giraffe on the wall were the perfect accents to complete the look.

Blog Update: April 25, 2010

I just love rainy Saturdays, especially when I'm at home enjoying it! Yesterday was such a special rainy day. We took a nice three hour nap and listened to the wonderful rainfall CD that the Lord played for us. After our hibernation ended, we cuddled on the couch to read a book for our Sunday school class. Chris read aloud and rubbed my stomach the entire time.

Ethan had been fairly quiet in his favorite spot on my lower left side for most of the day until this point. His little eleven ounce body rapidly rolled around toward the center of my belly. I interrupted Chris' reading to say, "Ethan is responding to your voice or your touch."

We both smiled and Chris continued to read. A few seconds later, Chris felt Ethan's little active body move for the first time. It was such a memorable moment. "Was that a kick?" Chris asked with the look of amazement.

"Either a kick or a high-five. He certainly wanted you to know that he hears you."

"Is this what you feel every day?"

"Yes, everyday; several times a day in fact."

"That was amazing," Chris said as he kissed my stomach and Ethan kicked him on the lips. "Alright Buddy, she was my wife before she was your momma. We have to share her."

I have tried with previous pregnancies to articulate how the movements felt, but nothing could compare to Chris actually feeling it for himself. So, this was the first movement he has EVER felt in four pregnancies!!!

I could almost predict that Ethan is gonna be a Daddy's boy! I couldn't believe him. I sing to him and he hears my voice all day and he doesn't respond to me like that! We've decided to start reading to him several times a week. I think it will be great bonding time for all of us! Maybe we can all learn from this. Listen for the voice of your Heavenly Father and respond accordingly!

Chapter 19
Milestone

We watched the calendar in anticipation of a milestone marking the longest period of time that we had been pregnant. After nineteen weeks, everything became new and I had no roadmap to reflect upon to alert me for what was to come. I made sure to use extra caution at work that day and not lift anything heavier than my purse. We even planned to have leftovers for dinner and used my lunch break to elevate my feet just as extra precaution. There were no signs that anything was going on out of the ordinary.

"Hey Babe, I just wanted to check on you and my baby boy before I left work. How are you feeling?" Chris asked cautiously.

"I feel great. Ethan has been practicing summersaults today, but we are fine."

"Alright, I'm on my way home. Do you need anything?'

"Just you! Now, hurry home to us."

My little gymnast and I curled up on the sofa and I immediately went to sleep. Ethan's practice sessions intensified, but I was able to rest through them.

"Hello everybody!" Chris roared, like jolly old St. Nick.

"Hey Daddy!" I whispered and tried to wake up from my refreshing power nap.

"Happy nineteen weeks, Babe!"

Rushing into the kitchen, I found him standing with a dozen beautiful red roses and a card.

"Aw, Babe! I..."

He interrupted and placed his free hand around my waist, "No, I wanted to celebrate us, and tell you thank you for your strength. You are amazing and I'm so thankful to share this joy with you."

I embraced his neck as tightly as possible and cried, which led to my happy sobbing. How could I not? His love had captured me in a special way. I was so honored to love him, be loved by him and give him as many children as he wanted to make. "Let me take a shower, I'm taking you to dinner. We have to make today extra special."

The days and weeks ahead passed at record speed. We submitted names and addresses to Tina for the first of four baby showers. Our families were hosting the inaugural event and they thought of every detail. They ensured everything was perfect and matched the nursery theme from the invitations, cake, and decorations down to the china and stemware used for the event.

"Tee, have the guest room ready for me. I am coming to this shower." Maxine advised. "I have to be there to celebrate with you and Chris and love on my little cousin."

"Max, you are going to fly down here just for a baby shower?"

"I most certainly am! There's no way that I wouldn't be there. I've already booked my flight and will arrive just after midnight on Friday," she informed me.

"No worries. I'll be there to get you," I said with a hint of excitement.

Nearly six years had passed since I'd seen Maxine. To say that we were glad to see each other was an understatement. There were so many old memories to catch up on: her successful career, how she manages a family, married life, and how much we miss Grandma. We laughed like teenagers until 3 a.m. We were deliriously exhausted. Our adrenaline levels were at an all time high. Surprisingly, when I woke up I felt completely rejuvenated. After a late breakfast, Maxine helped me decide on the perfect outfit for the shower. A spa pedicure for my swollen feet was the last order of business before arriving at the grand event.

The Pierre Estates, a historic mansion downtown, was beautifully decorated with fresh flowers, green and brown satin ribbon, and candles. The parking lot and both sides of the street were completely filled with guests for the shower. Chris and I were immediately overwhelmed by the multitude of well-wishers in attendance.

We were greeted with hugs and belly rubs! The first twenty minutes were spent mingling with the guests and thanking everyone for coming. Tina and Myra hosted several games while Momma and Jaye prepped the serving line which had been elegantly designed. Not a single detail was overlooked.

"Ohh's" and "ahh's," echoed throughout the mansion as we opened a mountain of gifts. "Where are we going to put all of this?" I inquired on several occasions.

"Don't worry, we'll find somewhere to put it." Chris smiled from ear to ear while opening a tiny outfit that read "Daddy's best friend."

The remaining showers were equally crafted with love and attention to detail. Lauren, Tenille, and other close friends hosted a co-ed shower at the upper level of The Marquee indoor Fun Park. And oh what fun we had watching Chris and his friends attempt to change the most dirty diapers in thirty seconds and participate in charades.

There were equal amounts of tears and laughter as we gathered to celebrate Baby Ethan's anticipated arrival. Charlie, the assistant at the dentist office, had become part of my inner circle and she was my personal comedian whenever I needed a laugh. She wanted to give the perfect gift, but couldn't find it in stores. Rather, the ideal gift was wrapped inside of her heart, one that also knew the horror of pregnancy loss and the joy of bringing a baby home. She wrote a poem about a mother's love for a child and many of the mothers in the room had tear-stained faces.

"Did you see your cake?" Lauren asked.

"Yes, thank you! I love it, especially the cup on the top layer that Ethan can use when he's older."

A quick reflection of light caught my eye as I hurriedly walked to the food table. "What was that?" I asked.

"What are you talking about?"

Closely investigated the cake, I thought to myself, *'I saw something.'*

"Maybe it was these angels," Lauren sincerely said with a smile.

There was a different sized silver angel charm placed on each layer of the cake for Destiny, Briauna, and Madison. An additional charm advertised the words: faith, hope, love. "I couldn't have something for Baby Ethan without acknowledging our girls also. The other charm is for you and Chris. I think it sums up how you've made it to where you are today," Lauren whispered.

While tightly hugging her neck, my tears met her lime green shirt. "Thank you! Thank you for remembering them. It means more to me than you'll ever know."

Chris arrived at the cake table just in time for Lauren to repeat the details. He was amazed at her thoughtfulness and proud of the recognition of his little girls' lives. The love that filled the room of The Marquee was irrefutable. The genuine expressions of excitement, sincere words penned in cards, and overwhelming joy that moved guests to tears reminded us of how fortunate we were to celebrate life and friendship.

Our living room looked like Santa had emptied several sleighs of goodies. Clothes, pampers, toys, huge boxes containing a stroller, crib, and car seat were piled high like fall leaves waiting for us to jump in. The visual chaos was thrilling. For the next several hours we organized the bounty, rearranged the nursery, and used the guest room closet to house the surplus. Thankfully we brought home a gallon of the punch that Tenille's mom made for the shower. The sugar rush kept the three of us energized and me in the bathroom.

Chapter 20
Babymoon & Showers of Blessings

The plans that we had thought about for years were becoming a reality. Although my knack for planning and strategizing was fairly precise, the ultimate realization of our dreams far exceeded anything imagined. With only a few weeks before Ethan's arrival, we felt the pressure to complete our to-do list without further delay. Every item on the list was important; however, the most essential task was to step away from everything and everyone to connect with each other again. At our core we were friends first and then lovers.

We loaded our red, two-door coupe with luggage and headed south on the freeway for a three day, two night babymoon. Conceptually, it's the same as a honeymoon except it happens before the baby arrives. The sunroof was open and the music mirrored that of our first date.

Laughter filled the car as we reminisced about old times and the anticipation of things to come. There were hardly any guests at the upscale bed and breakfast. We didn't mind having the entire property to ourselves. Our swim suits were quickly fetched from the unpacked luggage and twenty minutes after check-in, we were poolside, where we remained for several hours.

"Tomorrow you have a two hour massage scheduled at ten. My spa pedicure is at eleven and a facial at twelve fifteen. We can grab a quick lunch here and then get dressed for the photo session in the garden at three."

"That sounds good to me, but when are we going to rest?" Chris inquired.

"Rest? We'll rest tonight and all day tomorrow in the spa lounge before we check out, I promise."

The photographer, Elijah, was amazing. He wasn't there just to take pictures, but to create unforgettable memories. We shared our history of losses with him two weeks before the trip when we booked his services. He wanted to ensure that we had the first of many magnificent maternity photos. Elijah was honored to capture one of the happiest events of our lives.

"Be sure to bring several special props for our photo session," Elijah instructed me over the phone.

For clarification, I inquired, "Special props like what?"

"Bring things that belong to your husband, personalized gifts with your baby's name or initials, toys, stuffed animals. In fact, fill a bag with several items. We will be creative at the time of your session. You will not be disappointed."

We arrived at the terrace twenty minutes early to explore the scenery and examine locations for the photos. Elijah was already there and had staged scenic locations for various shots. He welcomed us with a hearty handshake and a wine glass of the best lemonade on this side of heaven. Thankfully, the sky was slightly overcast and there was a constant breeze making the July heat tolerable.

"Let's take a look at the items that you guys brought."

Chris pulled out a pocket watch, a pair of his dress shoes, a baseball glove, Bible and many other props for the session.

"Now, I don't know if you'll be able to use all of this, but we wanted to grab enough items," Chris informed Elijah.

"We'll have more than we need to complete an amazing shoot. There are also props along the path that you'll see. Let's get started by taking a walk toward the river. Just walk normally and I'll follow behind you."

We heard the sound of Elijah's camera snapping pictures rapidly as Chris reached for my hand. The thought of being watched and photographed made both of us snicker like mischievous kids. Our fast moving photographer had managed to position himself slightly in front of us just in time to capture the innocent kiss that Chris placed on my forehead.

Somehow, we forgot about the pictures and focused our attention on each other. Ethan must have become jealous and started his kickboxing sessions. Thankfully we were close to a bench where I could relax and prop my feet up. I lowered the blue band of my maternity jeans to expose all of the excitement. My overactive stomach was like a magnet and Chris's hands were the magnetic field. Elijah captured forty-five more minutes of beautiful memories of us and our playful exchanges with Ethan.

My favorite picture of the day was with the antique pocket watch which displayed 9:12 symbolizing Ethan's due date. Chris held the watch over my bare belly like a pendulum. The photo implied how swiftly time was moving toward the date of his anticipated arrival.

After our full day, we were, surprisingly, not exhausted. We laid down on the king-sized bed and made ourselves cozy under the overstuffed down comforter with intentions of taking a nap. Instead we held each other and talked about winning the lottery, living at the bed and breakfast, and being pampered every day. We ended the day by having a candlelight dinner downtown and a walk along the beach.

Reality welcomed us at the threshold of our home. We had no pool to retreat to, no housekeepers to make our bed, and certainly no masseuse. Someone had to clean the dust on the ceiling fans, wipe down our white kitchen cabinets and baseboards with bleach, and dust the furniture. Each evening I made minor progress in cleaning, but major progress in resting.

Chris spent his evening hours researching the internet for the perfect car for our growing family. My sports car would have to be parked because there was no way Ethan and all of his required belongs would fit in the small back seat. Nothing remotely met my approval. The minivans for sale were in abundance, but very few sports utility vehicles with a third row were available, at least not in our price range. There was no way I'd consent to being a minivan mom before the age of forty. Absolutely no way!

"Babe, we need to have a car purchased within the next two weeks. We're at week thirty-five and Dr. Halton plans to do the C-section at week thirty-eight. I'm afraid we'll run out of time."

"Don't worry; we'll have an SUV before Ethan is born. Trust me."

The anxiety of the growing to-do list and an overactive bladder kept me awake at night. So much so, that I resorted to cleaning the ceiling fans at three a.m. when Chris was sound asleep just to make progress. The cleaning obsession only escalated from day to day. Without warning, I had entered the nesting stage and nothing and no one, except Ethan of course, could stop me.

Our last follow up with Dr. Laurel was primarily to answer any questions pertaining to the surgery and what to expect during the stay. "Chris will be allowed in the operating room with us, right?"

"Yes, he'll be allowed in after we have successfully placed the epidural. During that time he can get dressed in scrubs and enjoy a few quiet moments before his life changes forever," Dr. Laurel explained. "Now, do either of you have any additional questions for me?

"Do you have a date scheduled yet?" Chris inquired.

Pointing to the wall calendar in the exam room, Dr. Laurel said, "I'm aiming for two weeks from Friday. Of course, this will all depend on your visit next week with Dr. Halton. You'll have a thorough ultrasound and as long as everything remains perfect, we're in good shape for Friday, September third."

"This has all gone by so fast. Seems like just a couple months ago I was calling to announce this pregnancy."

"Yes, it seems that way," Dr. Laurel agreed. "I have to tell you both that your tenacity and courage is impressive. All of us here at the office feel such happiness for you."

"Two weeks baby boy. Just hold on for two more weeks," whispered a very proud daddy as he drove me back to my office.

"I'm going to take a look around the car lot. I'll call you if I see anything interesting."

"Okay, remember we have two weeks from Friday. Two weeks."

"I promise we'll have an SUV with a third row before Ethan is born. Trust me," he repeated.

Impatience fueled my anxiety and the need to overly plan everything at work and at home. The subtle Braxton-Hicks contractions that I'd felt for some time had become painful. Clearly, my body was giving me warning notifications that the main event was soon to come.

My feet were very swollen. There was no separation between my ankles and feet. They all just merged together into one large trunk. In fact, everything was swollen. My hands were bare, because my wedding rings no longer fit. My nose stretched wide across my oily face. And of course, my stomach extended as big as the watermelons that grew in Grandma's garden. The twelve pounds that I had gained felt more like sixty. Despite each of the external attributes that I disliked, I felt beautiful and believed it when others told me so.

While looking at the bathroom mirror, I confidently said to myself, "You look amazing; absolutely amazing!" Seeing more than minor physical flaws, I had an up close and personal view of faith on display. Reflecting on the quality of my life over the prior two years, the resentment, anger, hopelessness, despair, and every other negative emotion had been cast away from my soul. All of my prior experiences helped me to fully embrace new experiences without reservation and fear. The best of times was before us.

For the first time, there were baby shower announcements posted at my job with my name on them. Seeing the bright yellow paper with teddy bears and building blocks made me so thankful and proud to be a mother, especially to a living baby. This would be the first shower that I attended where I didn't feel displaced. No one ever made me feel as if I didn't belong at the office showers. I simply didn't want my presence to dampen the mood or ignite fear in the mind of an expectant mother. It was much easier to leave my gift in the conference room before the guests arrived and exit the building.

My co-workers transformed our executive conference room into an inviting family space. There was a permanent smile painted on my face as I tried to contain the joy inside my heart. Many of the well-wishers in attendance had witnessed some of the most important and most difficult days of my life: engagement, wedding, four pregnancy announcements, three pregnancy losses, and an abundance of varying emotions in between.

The food table was beautifully decorated with fresh flowers, hors d'oeuvres, fruit, and cake squares with tiny blue booties from our favorite bakery. While savoring the cream cheese pound cake, I listened intently to the practical advice from co-workers, many of whom were mothers and had been for fifteen years or more. The most memorable tips were: "Always keep a camera close by. Ethan will change right before your eyes."

"Drink wine. You will be happier."

"Make some time for yourself. There will always be more laundry to fold and more chores to do. Just get to those things when you can."

"Snuggle with him as much as you can now. One day he'll grow up and you'll need these memories for when you really want to strangle him."

The massive undertaking of dismantling the mountain of gifts was solely my responsibility as Chris was at work and couldn't attend. Gifts were stacked nearly four feet high. I read every word of every card and nervously laughed away the tears of the heartfelt, written messages. We had an abundance of everything that we needed, except a car of course. I wondered how the gifts would fit into my sporty coupe.

"Thank you all so much for celebrating Baby Ethan with us. He is already surrounded by so much love and I can't wait to come back here to show him off. I appreciate the support that you've shown me over the years and I'm thankful that you all get to witness this miracle baby with us."

Chris had been told by his co-workers that they were hosting a shower for him, but he did not know when it would take place. He was surprised to learn it had been organized on the same day as my office shower. He left a voicemail message as my office shower concluded. "Babe, you will not believe what happened on our last break today. Call me when you get the message."

I called him as soon as I sat down in my jam-packed car. "Hey, I got your message. Is everything ok?"

"Yes ma'am, everything is fine. Would you believe that my co-workers hosted my shower today also?"

"Oh, that's awesome! I love that they recognize and celebrate daddies and not just mommas!"

"It was the greatest feeling ever. I can't describe it, but it was just good."

"I know the feeling you're talking about, because I felt the same way today. I didn't feel out of place, but genuinely celebrated for our present joy and not just remembered for our past pain."

"Precisely, that's exactly how I felt," Chris confidently stated.

Chris unpacked the bounty of gifts and piled them up like leaves in the living room floor. I wrote thank you cards while he put the items away. Two things were for sure: we were overwhelmed with love and completely out of space. Our home stood ready to receive the baby of our dreams. Designated closet space in the guest room and office had been converted into a well organized stock room.

Diapers were arranged by size and brand. Clothing was sorted by size, season, and color. Bottles had been washed and neatly lined up in the kitchen cabinets on parchment paper. Obviously, the nesting phase was in overdrive. However, I could not stop. Everything had to be perfect and in order for our son's homecoming.

There is still so much left to do before delivery day on Friday,' I thought as I slowly crawled into bed. As soon as my exhausted body landed comfortably between the silk sheets and my flannel blanket, I was well on my way to peaceful sleep. Unfortunately, the dust on the bedroom ceiling fan seemed to wave at me with each circular loop. The fan had to be cleaned before my body could have the rest that it desperately longed for.

I bolted out of bed and charged down the hallway to grab the duster from the laundry room before Chris heard me stirring about. The coast was clear and I was relieved that I didn't have to explain anything. The bedroom door was closed and locked as soon as I entered. I had a plan to execute and likely only a few minutes to do it well.

Towels were retrieved from the linen closet and placed on the bed to catch the dust. I staggered my way into a standing position on top of the bed and thoroughly cleaned all five blades. "Please don't let him come to the door," became my momentary request. The towels were thrown in the laundry basket and the duster returned to the laundry room without incident. I felt accomplished, relieved and finally ready for bed.

My coworkers were impressed to find thank you notes on their desk less than twenty four hours after the baby shower. Time was of the essence and no time could be wasted. The to-do list at work had been reviewed with a fine-tooth comb. I prepared a reference sheet of my responsibilities, disseminated it to my team and confirmed that my interim replacement felt confident in taking control of my assignments.

Intense abdominal pressure and back pain confirmed that the precise timing and level of preparation was on target. Several times throughout the day, my stomach would tighten as hard as a rock. Walking up and down the long, green carpeted hallway in the office seemed to ease the discomfort temporarily. Chris had called three times while I was away from the desk. I eased into my office chair and listened to his voicemail message. "Babe, where are you? Call me when you get back in the office. I am headed over your way."

"Hey, sorry that I missed your calls. Are you bringing lunch or something?" I asked out of breath.

"No, I don't have lunch, but I do have something that you want. Step outside for a minute."

"What is going on?"

Before he had a second to reply, I said, "Never mind, I'm coming."

The office door was quickly swung open. Marching down the laced concrete path, I looked for his navy blue truck. I scanned the parking lot again at a slower pace, but still could not find him. The sound of a very loud horn startled me and I quickly turned one hundred and eighty degrees to find Chris standing behind me. He was in my dream car! It was a midnight metallic SUV, fully loaded, with a sunroof and most importantly, a third row. "You found it!" I shouted, hugging his neck.

220

"Well, do you like it?" he asked as he motioned me to get in.

"Do I like it? No sir, I love, love, love it! This is big enough for two or three kids."

He had the sweetest grin on his face, which was probably the look of relief that he was free of my constant reminders. "I was fairly certain that you'd like this one. Do you want to take your lunch break now and take it for a quick drive to be sure?"

"Yes, I do! I'll be right back."

We made a few trips through the office parks nearby, but opted not to get on the freeway to avoid the noonday traffic. All of the buttons and gadgets worked. The vehicle was in excellent condition. Chris was seated in the back and checking out the second row features and flipping through the manual. Looking in the rearview mirror, I asked, "What do you think about it, Babe?"

"It's a good looking car. I believe that you'll be safe in here. Ultimately, I want to make sure this is what you want since you'll be driving it every day."

"But do you like it?" I emphasized.

"Yes, I do like it and if the paperwork can be completed today, this will be parked at our house tonight."

"Whoo hoo! Thank you; this is exactly what I've always wanted. If we do bring it home tonight, I want to get the car seat put in and have it loaded with our bags".

"We don't need to do that until next Thursday."

"No sir. I've been having a lot of pressure and back pain all morning. When I see Dr. Laurel tomorrow, I am doing whatever necessary to be admitted. An award winning, theatrical performance complete with crying and begging will be on display if I have to wait any longer."

"Do you think it's the real contractions?" he asked.

"Yeah, but mild ones, which is normal at thirty seven weeks."

"Shouldn't you call him now and go get checked just to be sure?"

"No, I still have things to get done. I don't need to be admitted yet."

Chris was visibly frustrated with my judgment, yet I held firm to my decision. My lunch break was almost over. I had not eaten a bite of food since the cinnamon raisin toast and peanut butter for breakfast. Somehow, my excitement suppressed my appetite.

Chris drove away in our soon-to-be new vehicle and I skipped back into the office. Nearly every item on the to-do list had been completed except packing our hospital bags and grocery shopping. Both of those tasks would take some time, but I was committed to stocking our house like a local supermarket.

Between the anxiety of what could be real labor and the anticipation of Chris's phone call to confirm our purchase, my concentration level was at an all time low. Thankfully, an afternoon meeting served as a welcomed intermission to the waiting game that was going on inside my head. After the meeting, I checked my voicemail and was elated to hear the official news that we had added a new car to our fleet. The courtesy van followed Chris home to drop off his truck while our new car was being washed and serviced. The second message, "Call me after your meeting," made me wonder if something had gone wrong.

Immediately I dialed his number. From the glee in his voice, I knew everything was fine. "Have you been outside lately?"

"No, why? Are you here?" I asked.

"I've already been there and now I'm on my way home."

Throwing my hands up in aggravation I asked, "Why didn't you wait for me? We could have picked up the SUV together!"

In his usual calm tone, he whispered, "The keys to the SUV are in your desk drawer in a brown envelope. I asked the receptionist to put them where you'd easily see them. I came by to drive your car home so that you could drive the SUV."

Laughter was being echoed on both ends of the phone. "How did I get so lucky to have a man like you? Thank you so much for making this happen."

"You're welcome. It's my pleasure. Are you coming straight home?"

"No way! I need to pick up some groceries. I am serious about being admitted to the hospital tomorrow."

"You are not going to the hospital tomorrow. Sounds like you need to come home and relax. I can make dinner," he suggested.

I gathered my belongings and hurriedly waddled my way onto the high driver's seat. The clean, fresh smell of leather, polished dashboard, and spotless interior made me feel like I had just purchased a brand new showroom model car. I rested my head on the headrest and slightly reclined my seat to relieve the pressure I felt from the waist down. With no time to waste, the ignition was started and I was on my way to purchase enough groceries to last two to three weeks.

By eight o'clock that evening, I had been to three stores getting anything that we'd possibly need as we settled into life as a family of three. Chris unloaded the groceries as I took a quick, well-deserved two minute break on the couch before returning to the kitchen to help him put things away. "Don't worry about the groceries. Just rest, I'll get them put away."

There was no argument coming from my lips. My body was finally getting what it had been asking for all day.

"Are you ready for dinner? I made a grilled chicken salad for you."

"Thank you, but I had a banana on the way home. I'll get the salad after I get our hospital bags packed. Have you packed?"

He laughed and asked, "For what? We are not going anywhere until Friday. I have plenty of time."

"Suit yourself. Just remember what I've told you. I am being extremely dramatic in the morning."

The rest break was over. Ethan's designer diaper bag, which was a gift from Summer and Joe, was assembled. A surplus of outfits, lotions, burp cloths, socks, nightgowns, mittens, hats, gloves and anything else that could fit into the bag were added. The bag was filled to capacity. Chris had to suppress the sides in order for me to struggle to close the zipper.

Most of my necessities were already on the guest bed. Little by little, I started dropping my hospital items on the bed several weeks prior. My honest intentions of having the bag packed well in advance failed. However, I was determined to finish the task quickly. After adding my toiletries, camera, extra phone charger and batteries, my bag was packed and ready to be loaded in the car.

"Babe, did you put the car seat in already?"

"I have the base in. I started on the seat, but it's too dark outside. I can't see where all of the straps go. I'll look at it tomorrow."

"Tomorrow?!" I asked sarcastically.

"Yes, tomorrow. I'm headed to bed; it's already eleven o'clock. I've already made my lunch, so don't worry about making it."

"Can you at least put my bag, Ethan's bag, and the banner in the car before you go to bed?"

"What banner?"

"The announcement for the door that I ordered months ago. Remember?"

"Vaguely. What does it say?

"Babe, it's the yellow banner with the rubber ducks on it. It says Chris and Tanika proudly welcome Baby Christopher Ethan into our hearts and home or something similar to that."

"Oh yeah, I remember."

"I want something more than the traditional blue ribbon saying, "It's a boy" on our door."

"The bags will be fine. I'll take care of everything when I get off tomorrow. Come on, take your shower and get ready for bed," he requested.

"On my way, Sir."

The pressure that I felt most of the day had only intensified during the evening. There was simply no time to stop and focus on the discomfort. A steaming, hot shower was precisely what my back needed to feel momentary relief. The tension in my body was being washed down the drain. After nearly a thirty minute shower, the water grew cold and I was forced out of my spa haven into our warm bed.

"Goodnight Lil Buddy. Are you ready to sing your ABC's?" Chris asked while rubbing my belly.

"I believe he's asleep. The hot shower likely calmed him down. He's had a very long day."

"What was that?" he asked abruptly.

"That's the pressure and vibrations that I've felt all day. I believe they are mild contractions."

"I actually felt your stomach tighten up and then release. That was amazing. Does it hurt?"

"It's more discomfort than pain. This could go on for days. It's nothing to be concerned about until they are three minutes apart."

Chris sang the ABC's to Ethan as was the custom. Somewhere between A and Z his peaceful, velvet voice lulled me to sleep. Assuredly, the song was followed by bedtime prayers and blessings. My eyes sprang open when he concluded with, "Amen."

"Amen and good night," I mumbled.

Chapter 21
For Unto Us

My sound sleep was disrupted by a very active bladder. The clock displayed 1:18 a.m. Thankfully, there were several hours more to sleep before Chris's alarm sounded at a quarter after five. I happily pulled the covers around my neck and tried to sleep although I continued to feel the contractions. "Babe!" I screamed as I pulled on Chris' arm to wake him. "Something is happening. I need some towels, quick."

He moved like lightening to grab towels from the linen closet. Frantically he replied, "What are you feeling?"

After grinding my teeth and clenching my pillow to counter the pain, I panted, "I think... (deep breath) he's coming. I'm actually hurting now."

"Can you feel Ethan moving? Is he okay?"

"I can't feel…. (deep breath) anything except pain right now."

"Should I call Dr. Laurel or Halton?"

"Laurel, but first can you help me to the shower? The hot water helped earlier. We can try that before we call."

As soon as I rolled over to exit the bed, there was one loud popping noise followed by a gush of water. "That's my water! My water just broke!!!" I shouted and nervously laughed. "I'll page Dr. Laurel when I get out of the shower. We're about to have a baby! Start packing your bags!"

Chris's feet were glued to the floor and his eyes were stretched in amazement. "Christopher!!!"

Clapping my hands to get his attention, "Christopher Dillard!!! Pack your bags, Sir."

"Wow, I cannot believe it's finally time," he said, while moving at a bewildered pace.

The shower provided little relief. In fact, the contractions were four minutes apart. There was no time to spare. Dr. Laurel returned my page and instructed us to meet him on the fourth floor of the hospital. As soon as the operating room could be scheduled, he'd perform the c-section.

In record time Chris moved from slow gear to overdrive. All of our bags were in the car and the bed linens were stripped after I disconnected with Dr. Laurel. "Are you ready to go get our boy and bring him home?"

Barely lifting my head from my chest, I whispered, "Yes, but not until this contraction is over."

Chris wrapped his strong arms around my tensed body until I stood upright. Our eyes met and tears of joy and fear fell simultaneously. He soothed my anxious heart with his faith-filled words, just as he'd done many times before. "Our finest hour is upon us. We can do this with God's help."

Before leaving home, I left a voicemail message at Chris's job to report his absence. A text message to my supervisor with the latest developments was sent. *"My water broke at 2:10 a.m. We're on our way to the hospital."*

An immediate response of, *"I'm saying a prayer for all of you. Please update us when you can,"* appeared on my phone.

We drove in silence except for my intermittent moaning during contractions and his spontaneous prayer. Chris maneuvered the wheel with his left hand and rubbed my stomach with his right hand. There were no cars on the road, yet our car moved at the pace of someone taking a sightseeing tour through the countryside. In my mind, I was yelling, *"Speed up for goodness sakes! I'm in labor!"* However, my heart cautiously challenged me to savor every second of this new experience.

By the time I decided to follow the leading of my heart, we were at the hospital. We were already preregistered thanks to the advice from Dr. Laurel's staff. At the nurses' station we were greeted with hugs from the staff that had come to know us well over the years. "Welcome back!" Drew said as she patted Chris on the shoulder. "Let's go to room 437 to get you ready to have this baby."

I was beyond relieved that we bypassed room 439. "Here's your gown. Make sure that you remove all of your jewelry and put them in your suitcase. If you don't mind, I'm going to ask you questions while you undress. Dr. Laurel will be here any minute now and I don't want to keep him waiting."

"Sure, that's fine," I agreed.

"When was the last time you ate or drank?"

"Water at 10:30 and a banana about 7:00."

"Any medications other than your prenatal vitamins and baby aspirin?"

"No, that's all."

"And you do not have a latex allergy, correct?"

"That's correct."

"Let's get this monitor on so that we can see your contractions and listen to this anxious baby."

The pale pink Velcro straps were tightly secured around my round, vibrating stomach. Drew squirted warm gel on the probe touching my stomach and we immediately heard the strong, rapid heartbeat that we'd been listening to for months. Our little miracle baby was peacefully resting. Perhaps he knew that a good nap was in order before the main event.

"I have a consent form for you to sign, stating that we have your permission to give you blood or blood products in the event you require them. I'm sure you're familiar with this."

"Yes, I remember this," I said as I signed the electronic signature pad.

"That's all I need from you, everything else is in the chart. Someone from the lab will be in shortly to draw your blood and then anesthesia should be up to get your IV started. I remember how much trouble we had last time and we're not putting you through that again."

"Thank you so much. I appreciate that," Chris said from the chair beside my bed.

Everything went as planned. A record was broken as the lab tech accessed my only good, magical vein the first time. After an apologetic third attempt, the IV was successfully placed in my right hand. Surely the stars were in perfect alignment.

Once the hustle settled down, Chris slipped on the blue, paper thin surgical outfit and made the calls to our mothers and sisters. From across the room I could hear Momma scream and shout, "I'm on my way right now!" My mother in law, Angie, assured Chris that she'd be praying for us and instructed him to call when Ethan arrived.

"Good morning. Dr. Laurel here," echoed a soft voice as the hospital room door opened.

"Good morning. I couldn't wait until 9:00 to see you."

"I see. This little guy is anxious to meet you today."

"And we are just as anxious to meet him," Chris said proudly.

"You're having some very strong and regular contractions I see," Dr. Laurel said as he reviewed the printout from the monitor.

"The OR team is ready for us. We can all head that way in a few minutes. You will get your epidural in the OR and then someone will step out to get Chris from the waiting area."

"That sounds good to me," I said.

"Do either of you have questions for me?"

"My cerclage will remain in place, right?"

"Yes, I won't have to touch the cerclage at all. Typically, it's never removed, unless it causes you problems."

I was briskly wheeled down the long, bright hallway with Chris by my side. This time my head wasn't buried in my chest and my eyes were wide open. An overwhelming feeling of fortitude and strength filled my soul as I reflected on our journey in and out of the hospital over the years. Finally, we had arrived at the place where we'd greet the long awaited, highly anticipated object of our affection.

"Chris, we will let you give her a kiss and then you can relax and wait for us here while she gets the epidural. It won't take long," Drew instructed as she tied the white strings of the sterile cap behind her head.

A tight hug was followed by three soft kisses on my lips. "I'll see you soon, Babe. Be brave."

"Love you!" I whispered while choking back tears.

The OR attendant checked my ID bracelet and had me verify the last four digits of my social security number before entering the arctic surgical suite. The staff worked together effortlessly without instruction to position me onto the narrow operating table.

The tiny-framed nurse became my drill sergeant. "Put your hands around my shoulders. You're going to feel three cold wipes down your back," Drew instructed.

"Now, hold still and point your toes to the floor while arching your back out."

I followed the instructions precisely. "Here comes a little pressure, just hold still. You're doing great."

"Relax. Breathe normally," Drew said calmly.

The anesthesiologist reported, "We are all done."

Within minutes, my lower body was completely numb. The surgical techs were counting their instruments aloud while a cool fan was being positioned at my head. My arms were strapped to the table and an oxygen mask was applied to my face. Chris strolled into the room with his eyes stretched wide open. He was amazed at the number of people in the room and all of the equipment necessary to get the baby out.

One of the attendants said, "Chris, you can have a seat on this stool right beside Tanika."

His sweaty palms immediately started rubbing my head. "How are you feeling?"

"Hot!"

"Is this fan helping?"

"A little, but your warm, slippery hands aren't helping either."

"Oh, sorry," he said with a smile.

"Can you feel anything?"

"I know he's started, because I can feel just a little pressure, but not any pain. What were you doing in the waiting room?"

"Waiting for someone to come get me. Seemed like I was in there for an hour. I also called Cynthia and left a message on her office phone that we're here."

"Thank you. I thought about that earlier, but didn't get a chance to call."

Dr. Laurel's voice sounded from behind the blue screen, "Tanika, you're doing great. I've cut through your previous incision line and can see the cerclage is still in place. Looks like we'll have this baby out in no time."

"Great, thank you," I replied as Chris and I both looked at each other with excitement.

"It's 5:40 – I predict he'll arrive at 5:47,"Chris announced.

"I just know he's coming sooner rather than later."

We overheard muffled chatter behind the blue screen, but couldn't decipher the details of the conversation. Drew appeared from the side of the sterile shield and asked, "Dad would you like to see Baby Ethan's entrance into the world?"

Without hesitation he replied, "No ma'am, there's no one to catch me if I faint on the floor."

"Well, get your camera ready. He'll be screaming hello to you in a few seconds."

While quickly shifting from left to right on the stool, he proclaimed," I'm ready!"

With eyes fixed on the tranquil blue drape covering my body, I held my breath until Ethan had taken his first breath. The movement in the room accelerated while all of the chatter came to an abrupt halt. An unfamiliar voice calmly shouted, "5:42."

In the same millisecond, Drew commanded, "Dad, stand up on the count of three. 1, 2... Before she could conclude, the room was filled with the most beautiful, delicate cry that had ever passed our ears. Dr. Laurel's calm, monotone voice was exchanged for a triumphant declaration, "And here he is!" while displaying Ethan just above the barrier that separated us. His plump body covered in a thick, white coating and stained with blood was a beautiful sight to behold.

Chris quickly emerged from his seat to welcome and honor the entrance of his beloved son and namesake. His trembling voice proudly echoed through the operating room, "That's my boy, that's *my* boy. Hi, Lil Buddy!"

Before I counted his ten tiny fingers or toes, I concluded. "He is absolutely perfect."

Ethan's delicate cry immediately ceased when he heard the voice of the one who had guided him since his earthly beginning. He was whisked away by the staff as Dr. Laurel put my body back together. We had become parents to a full term, healthy, seven pound, two ounce baby. Nothing--not one thing--could compare to the overwhelming joy of seeing, hearing, and soon holding the dream that had become a reality.

Chris reclaimed his seat and kissed my tear-stained face. "Thank you, Lord." he whispered in appreciation.

"Yes, thank you Lord for our precious boy," I echoed.

Our thankful hearts soon turned to impatient hearts. "How much longer will it be before I can hold him?" Chris quietly asked me.

"Shouldn't be long. He has to pass his newborn testing and get cleaned up first. Just be patient, we'll have a lifetime to hold him."

"Something came over me and I didn't even get a picture of him."

"Something like what, tears?" I asked, but he didn't respond.

Drew called out from the incubator in the rear of the room, "I'm coming with this cute little baby just as soon as I get his footprints."

As soon as we heard her footsteps, Chris pulled out both cameras, dropped them on my bed and extended his arms to embrace his boy. There were no words spoken, for they would have been inadequate to show the adoration and relief that hid behind Chris' infectious smile. His hands looked enormous as he gently stroked Ethan's jet black, silk-like hair.

Chris lowered Ethan so that we were cheek to cheek. "Here's Mommy, say hi."

His bright eyes were wide open and seemed to illuminate the operating room. "I'm so happy to see you and can't wait to hold you."

The next thirty minutes were spent with an emesis basin under my clammy face, a cool towel on my head, and anti-nausea medicine through my IV. Ironically, I completed thirty seven weeks of pregnancy without the slightest hint of nausea or morning sickness, but that carefree experience was over. I felt horrible and lifting my head from the paper thin pillow seemed to be impossible.

"Tanika, we've got you all fixed up. The closure took a little more time than expected, because there is some scar tissue from your cerclage placement, but you should heal up just fine."

"Thank you so much Dr. Laurel. You've seen us through our worst and now our best days," I said.

"You're welcome. It's my pleasure. Let's get you into a comfortable bed and wheeled back to your room. I know you're anxious to hold this little guy."

"Yes sir, I am."

Chris moved as if he were handling fine china as he delicately placed Ethan in bed with me. "Are you going to be all right to hold him or do you want me to?"

"No, I'm fine."

Well, I was fine until the bed started to move at the speed of light down the hall. I slammed my eyes shut and clinched Ethan like a football under my arm until we arrived safely at room 439. Our postpartum nurse, Jodi, was waiting on us to arrive and received a detailed report from Drew. While they talked, Chris sat on the bed with me while I held our baby boy and sang sweet lullabies. He was bundled up in the blue and pink hospital blanket, but it was important to us that he felt and heard what was familiar to him.

The blanket was stripped off and he was securely nestled on my chest. Chris and I both covered his back with our bare hands to keep him warm. We caressed his smooth body until he was sound asleep. "Can I get anything for either of you? Mom, you can have popsicles, jello, ice chips, and clear liquids. And Dad, you can have whatever you'd like," Jodi asked.

"I'd love ice water and a popsicle, please."

"And I'll have coffee with cream and sugar if you don't mind. Can I also have some tape to hang a banner on our door?"

There was a knock at the door followed by an immediate opening. "Good morning," Momma sang in a high soprano voice.

"Hey Momma, don't you look pretty all dressed up in your blue suit."

She dropped her purse and hugged the both of us tightly. "Look at my Angel boy! He is beautiful," she said as she wiped tears on her handkerchief.

"Thank you. You can hold him if you want. He's been asleep on my chest for awhile."

Cynthia visited us as soon as she received Chris's message. She was just as much a part of our family as those who shared our DNA. Suzanna's visit was most special. She entered our room with her beautiful brown eyes filled with tears and a smile painted on her face. After a long hug to Chris and me, she washed her hands and said, "I need to hold him. You know that this is *my* baby?"

"Yes, Suzanna. I will share him with you. After all that you've done for us, I couldn't think of a more perfect birthday gift than to have him on your birthday."

"This sweet boy is the answer to many, many prayers. He is such a miracle," Suzanna said as she stroked Ethan's tiny nose.

Our room was filled with family, friends, and staff all day. Ethan was greeted with everything from happy tears, to soft kisses on his cheek, to gentle pats on his bottom. The list of well-wishers was endless; Tina, Myra, Lauren, Dominique, Tenille, Jaye, Mrs. Angie, Summer, Joe, Charlie, Daddy, Dr. Halton and others.

He was amazingly cute and was the perfect blend of both of us. His nose, cheeks, and lips mostly resembled Chris. The paintbrush-like fingers and long extremities were from me. The silky, jet black hair however, reminded me most of Grandma's Indian hair.

Momma and Pop Dawkins arrived just in time to assist Chris with Ethan's first bath. Chris announced, "I'm nervous. I've never held a baby this small before."

"You'll be fine, Son," Momma Dawkins reassured him. "I'll be right here to help if you need me. I won't let you hurt our new grandbaby," she said while slowly rubbing her hand across his back.

Obviously, Ethan did not care for the water and commenced screaming louder than he did in the delivery room. "Daddy's sorry Lil' Buddy. I'm just trying to get you all cleaned up."

The magic of Daddy's voice proved incapable of being the magical soothing agent in this instance. Pop Dawkins assured Chris, "This is normal. Most kids have this response to baths for the first few weeks. Don't worry, Son, you're doing just fine."

Perhaps hearing those words from his father figure gave him the confidence that he needed. He stood upright, squared his shoulders and moved with confidence to finish. Momma Dawkins helped him wash Ethan's hair and dress him in the blue and brown striped outfit that my Daddy gave us.

The next day was eventful. Hearing screening, shots, and circumcision in a very short span of time wore thin on my patience. The silver lining that day was our session with the newborn photographer. Ethan's beautiful brown eyes were wide open for every click of the camera. The most amazing picture of the session was of Ethan lying peacefully in Chris's palms. His tiny hand gripped Chris's index finger. My proud husband and Ethan's affectionate father softly kissed his cheek precisely as the camera captured the award winning image.

As much as we enjoyed the conveniences of the hospital for the previous two days, we were eager to introduce Ethan to his home. More importantly, I wanted to actually rest without interruptions for lab work and blood pressure checks around the clock. The on-call pediatrician was reluctant to discharge us because he suspected Ethan might be developing jaundice. There was a lab result that was slightly below normal. We had three options: send him to the neonatal intensive care unit for light therapy, discharge him and expose to natural light, or remain in the hospital with no intervention until a firm diagnosis was made. We opted to take our baby boy home and give him all of the sunlight that he could handle.

For the first time, we were leaving the hospital with life and the anticipation of memories yet to be made. Our heads were held high as we stopped to greet strangers in the hallway who wanted to wish us well. We didn't mind the delay and embraced the opportunity to inspire others by telling about our miracle baby.

Jodi pushed my wheelchair onto the cobblestone hospital entrance. With her hand gently on my shoulder she said, "Go home and spoil this baby. I want to see you guys back in here in another year doing this all over again."

"I can promise you that we will be back. However, I cannot promise you that it will be as soon as you'd like. Give us at least eighteen months."

Chris carefully secured Ethan's car seat in the harness as I captured pictures of his every step. With Jodi's assistance, I slowly maneuvered my way into the back seat. "It's been my pleasure to take care of all of you. You have such a beautiful family."

We replied in unison, "Thank you so much."

Our family was finally on the way home. Chris chauffeured us as if he had the most precious cargo in tow. Our car never accelerated to the acceptable sixty-five miles per hour on the freeway. We were in the slow lane of life and happily enjoying all of the scenery along the way. The safari-themed car seat seemed to engulf Ethan's tiny body. Even with a head support, his head still managed to fall forward. With one hand, I propped his head and rubbed his feet with the other until we arrived at home.

Chris opened the car door, paused to look at us briefly and kissed my cheek. He was speechless, but the innocent smile on his face spoke for itself. He wanted to scream with joy as he escorted us across the threshold of our home.

"Let's get him out of this seat and I'll get the bags later."

After no less than ten repetitive kisses from Chris, he was placed in my arms. We slowly walked Ethan through his new home. "This is your nursery Lil' Buddy. Do you see the yellow lion and the tall, brown giraffe?"

Our boy was comfortably asleep for the duration of the tour, but that did not stop us from introducing him to each room in the house. The last stop of the tour was our bedroom. My cozy bed seemed to draw my sore body in closer. "Will you bring the bassinet in here? I'm going to take a nap while he's asleep."

"Yes, I'll be right back," Chris said while moving swiftly to the nursery.

"Are you going to lie down with us?'

"No, I have too much to do," he replied.

Ethan slept peacefully in his bassinet. After closely watching him a few minutes, my eyes struggled to remain open. The feel of cold, silk sheets combined with a thick, flannel blanket was just what I needed to go right to sleep. After nearly two hours, I opened my eyes to the delight of Ethan's deep brown eyes watching me. Thankfully, he wasn't crying but he was attempting to suck three fingers at once. My breast nursed him until he was satisfied.

While we slept, Chris had unpacked our belongings, started laundry, and found time to nap on the couch. The banner that once hung on our hospital door was now over our fireplace. Although it did not match our great room's brown and gold color scheme, it was the perfect accent to the room. And so were the swing, play mat, and bouncer that were set up in the area. The once cold, spacious room was filled with vibrant color, warmth, and life. Ethan was such a calm baby. He rarely cried and once he was fed and changed, he returned to his peaceful state, which made for an uncomplicated first night at home.

"Don't forget that we need to give him natural sunlight. Should we go out before it gets too hot?" I asked.

"Yes, why don't we eat breakfast and then go?"

Ethan was stripped down to a diaper and we began walking toward the sun just before ten o'clock. The birds were beautifully singing a celebratory tune as we inched along the street. Suddenly a yellow butterfly circled our heads and flew between our shoulders. Before either of us could say a word, another majestic, yellow butterfly swooped down and joined the first. "Oh my goodness! Look! There are three yellow butterflies now," I shouted softly in amazement as I made a complete U-turn in the middle of the street.

"Incredible! Absolutely incredible," Chris whispered.

Without question, we saw those creatures as heartfelt representatives of Destiny, Briauna, and Madison. Perhaps they were furloughed from heaven in the form of butterflies so that for the first time we could all be together as a family--a living, breathing, energetic family. They were distinctive symbols of faith, hope, and love; of our past, our present, and our beautiful future. After a spectacularly choreographed performance concluding with the wing of a butterfly tenderly brushing Ethan's back, they flew away one by one towards the rising sun.

The most wonderful time of the year had arrived in a different season than expected. In those brief moments intended to expose Ethan to sunlight, we received a shower of healing balm for our hearts accompanied by the blessing to build a family that would sustain our once broken hearts.

Epilogue

The joys of motherhood came with many added bonuses. From the moment Chris held Ethan's 7lb 2oz body upon his shoulder, I instantly fell deeper in love with him. His eyes conveyed the magic I saw on our first date and at our wedding. It was intense, purposeful gazing with a message of gratitude and pride. Not only was I in love, but he too was completely smitten with his namesake.

Chris was raised without an active father in his life, but innately knew how to care for his child. The lion-like nature in him intently watched over Ethan as he slept, while the lamb-like nature in him greeted Ethan with numerous kisses every time he opened his eyes. Although we were parents from the moment two lines appeared on the pregnancy test, this was the first time we were able to parent a child.

We naturally developed our routine. Chris would pray the Scriptures over Ethan each night and I'd give him five goodnight kisses. He received a kiss for himself, Destiny, Briauna, Madison, and an extra kiss for anyone who needed it in heaven. Ethan was our angel and we were certain he communicated with his sisters and could easily pass on our love to them.

We both walked proudly with squared shoulders as we introduced Ethan to our friends and family. His life was a tangible testament of unrelenting faith, hope for the discouraged, and the faithfulness of our God. Finally, we were writing a new chapter in our lives and filling each page with love.

The holiday season was filled with many firsts: Ethan's first Thanksgiving, first taste of sweet potato pie, first picture with Santa and most excitedly, our first "happy" Christmas since 2006 when we married. Our Thanksgiving was reminiscent of times past when everyone gathered at Grandma's house and filled it with love. Having a newborn baby, I thought, would exempt me from making my usual contributions of ham, potato salad, banana pudding, and lemonade to the meal. Surely, snuggling with my bright-eyed baby boy outweighed meal preparation. However, the anticipation in my nephew's voice over the phone clearly indicated he expected his banana pudding with extra crackers and very few bananas.

While Ethan caught up on his sleep, I prepared my portion of the meal. We gathered at Grandma's house and in between setting the table, I refereed whose turn it was to hold Ethan. He was passed around more than the side dishes. Our contribution to the meal was so much more than food. We brought joy to our family gathering and shared him without reservation.

We decorated our tree and home just days after Thanksgiving. Our handsome, four month old son was one of the best gifts, and certainly the cutest, we'd ever received. We had an impromptu photo session at home and dressed jolly ole Ethan in a red Santa's helper outfit and placed him under the sparkling tree. His presence eliminated the need for presents. His bright smile and infectious laugh filled our home and our days with a joy that we have never known.

"He is perfect, Babe," Chris said.

"Yes, he absolutely is."

BUILDING A FAMILY BREAKS MY HEART

www.ingramcontent.com/pod-product-compliance
Lightning Source LLC
Chambersburg PA
CBHW061637040426
42446CB00010B/1458